America Speaks
THE BIRTH OF THE NATION

VOLUME
9

WOMEN

Jane Penrose

GROLIER

First published in the United States in 2005 by
Grolier, a division of Scholastic Library Publishing,
Sherman Turnpike, Danbury, CT 06816

For Compendium Publishing
Series editor: Don Gulbrandsen
Picture research: Jane Penrose and Sandra Forty
Design: Tony Stocks/Compendium Design
Artwork: Mark Franklin

Printed in China through Printworks Int. Ltd.

Library of Congress Cataloging-in-Publication Data
    p. cm.
Summary: "Recounts the making of America until 1815 through
the eyes and voices of ordinary people"—Provided by publisher.
Includes indexes.

Contents: v. 1. Merchants / Angus Konstam—v. 2.
Manufacturers / Wayne Youngblood—v. 3. Armed Forces / Ian
Westwell—v. 4. Transporters / John Westwood—v. 5.
Professionals / Marcus Cowper—v. 6. Workers / Marcus Cowper
—v. 7. Underprivileged / Duncan Clarke—v. 8. Lawmen and
Lawbreakers / Philip Wilkinson—v. 9. Women / Jane Penrose—
v. 10. Children / Jane Penrose.

ISBN 0-7172-6030-5 (set : alk. paper)—ISBN 0-7172-6020-8 (v. 1
: alk. paper)—ISBN 0-7172-6021-6 (v. 2 : alk. paper)—ISBN 0-
7172-6022-4 (v. 3 : alk. paper)—ISBN 0-7172-6023-2 (v. 4 : alk.
paper)—ISBN 0-7172-6024-0 (v. 5 : alk. paper)—ISBN 0-7172-
6025-9 (v. 6 : alk. paper)—ISBN 0-7172-6026-7 (v. 7 : alk. paper)
—ISBN 0-7172-6027-5 (v. 8 : alk. paper)—ISBN 0-7172-6028-3
(v. 9 : alk. paper)—ISBN 0-7172-6029-1 (v. 10 : alk. paper)

1. United States—History—Colonial period, ca. 1600-1775—
Sources—Juvenile literature. 2. United States—History—
Revolution, 1775-1783—Sources—Juvenile literature. 3. United
States—History—1783-1815—Sources—Juvenile literature. 4.
United States—Social conditions—To 1865—Sources—
Juvenile literature. I. Konstam, Angus.

E188.A495 2005
973.2'5—dc22

                                                    2005040309

ACKNOWLEDGMENTS

The photographs in this book came from
the following sources. Numbers refer to
pages

Corbis: 1 (Bettmann/Corbis), 5 (Geoffrey
Clements/Corbis), 10 (David Muench/
Corbis), 11 (Raymond Gehman/Corbis),
12 (Bettmann/Corbis), 13 (Richard T.
Nowitz/Corbis), 25 (Bettmann/Corbis), 26,
27 (Bettmann/Corbis), 28, 29 (Bettmann/
Corbis & Corbis), 30A (North Carolina
Museum of Art/Corbis), 31 (Bettmann/
Corbis), 40A (Bettmann/Corbis), 42A
(Bettmann/Corbis), 43 (Bettmann/Corbis),
44 (Franklin McMahon/Corbis &
Bettmann/Corbis), 45 (Bettmann/Corbis),
46B, 58 (Bettmann/Corbis), 65 (Bettmann/
Corbis), 68 (Hanan Isachar/Corbis &
Seattle Art Museum/Corbis), 69
(Bettmann/Corbis), 71 (Bettmann/Corbis).
Getty Images: 3 (all), 4, 6 (both), 8 (Time
Life Pictures/Getty Images), 9, 14 (both),
16 (both), 17, 18 (both), 19 (Time Life
Pictures/Getty Images), 20, 21 (both), 22,
23 (both), 24 (both), 30 (below), 32
(both), 33, 34A (above), 35, 36 (both), 37
(both), 38 (both), 40B (below), 41, 42B
(below), 46A (above), 47, 48 (both), 49, 50,
51 (both), 54 (both), 55, 56 (both), 55, 56
(both), 57, 59, 60 (both), 61 (all), 62
(both), 63, 64 (Time Life Pictures/Getty
Images), 66, 67, 69B (below), 70, 72, 73.
Richard Hook: 34 (below).

CONTENTS

Baptism of Virginia Dare.

LEFT: **This modern painting shows what the baptism of Virginia Dare might have looked like. Virginia was born on August 18, 1587, on Roanoke Island, now in North Carolina. She was the first child of English parents to be born in North America and the granddaughter of the colony's governor, John White. No one knows what happened to Virginia, since the colony and its inhabitants vanished mysteriously and became known as the "Lost Colony."**

RIGHT: **"Hail, Bright Aurora" by an unknown American artist about 1815.**

The history of a nation is made up of many parts and many people. Each has a story to tell, and it is the historian's job to find these stories, to read them, and to understand what they can tell us about the time in which they were written.

In the history of America the role played by women is as important as that played by men. However, the history of women is often harder to find. For centuries women and men were treated very differently, and the history books often reflect only the words and deeds of men. To put together a history of America, from the arrival of the first settlers to the Revolutionary War, the words, thoughts, and actions of women must be explored, too.

Primary sources
In this book you will learn, through primary sources, about the daily lives and work of many different women in early America. Primary sources are those that come straight from the horse's mouth, so to speak. They are the diaries, letters, books, pamphlets—even the shopping lists—of the people who lived at the time. Primary sources are often the most

reliable records of history, because people who were actually there wrote them, and they could see what was going on. When studying women's history, however, it is important to remember that fewer women could write than men at this time, and women were less likely than men to write down important events in their lives. Most journal writers were men, and men wrote most books at this time. Sources written by men are very useful for finding out what men thought of women, but they are not good for discovering the true thoughts and opinions of women. For this the student of women's history must look further afield.

Women's stories are sometimes told in their own words, through diaries, letters, and memoirs. More often, however, their history must be pieced together from documents written by men, regarding how women should behave, how they should (or, more often, should not) be educated, their achievements, and their crimes. All of these documents are important to the historian, but the natural bias in each must be remembered, to keep them from being misleading.

Native and African American women
Within the study of women's history in early America, primary sources from Native American and African American women are very rare. Some Native American societies were literate, but few documents remain from these groups. Most women who arrived from Africa were illiterate, and very few were taught to read or write as slaves. This makes the historian's job harder, because the history of these people must be studied through the documents produced by European settlers at this time. The relationship between Native Americans or African Americans and the European settlers was not often a fair one, so the primary sources available must be used carefully. They will tell us what white, European settlers—usually men—knew and thought about Native American and African American women, but nothing about what those women themselves thought about their own lives or the people around them.

Rich and poor
Wealthy women were more likely to write things down than their poorer cousins.

THE YOUNG LADIES' LITERARY SOCIETY

Questions Discussed in the Society, with their Decisions as given by the acting President. Commencing in the summer of 1813

No. 1: Is the curiosity of the sexes equal? Decided in the Affirmative [yes]
No. 4: Do novels produce more evil than good? Affirmative
No. 5: Does pride produce more good than evil? Affirmative
No. 6: Is fashion productive of more good than evil? Affirmative
No. 8: Are Thanksgivings advantageous? Affirmative
No. 10: Are Female Literary Societies advantageous? Affirmative
No. 11: Can a state of equality exist in Society? Negative [no]
No. 20: What vice is most hurtful? Drunkenness
No. 22: What is the greatest virtue? Charity
No 24: Is happiness equally distributed among the different orders of society? Negative
No 28: Do Spectres [ghosts] exist? Negative
No 31: Does it appear from reason that the soul is immortal? Affirmative
No 34: Does poverty produce more misery than wealth? Affirmative
No 42: What is the principal cause of evil in society? Defective Education
No 44: Is assassination ever justifiable? Negative.
No 45: Does it appear from reason that man can be justified in taking the lives of inferior animals? Negative
No 46: Are men more prone to evil than good? Affirmative
No 47: Are the heroic virtues commendable in females? Affirmative
No 54: Do females enjoy more happiness than males? Negative
No 57: Ought novel reading to be prohibited by law? Affirmative
No 58: Is a cultivated mind necessary to domestic happiness? Affirmative
No 65: Ought ladies to endeavour to excel in the sciences? Negative.
No 66: Ought a female ever to rule a nation? [no answer]

Not only were wealthy women more likely to be educated, and therefore literate, than poorer women, but they also had more time to devote to letter writing or to joining literary societies. The life experiences of wealthy women were different from those of poorer women of the same period, but some of their opinions on what is right and wrong are likely to be the same. For this reason the writings of a group of young women in Deerfield, Massachusetts, serve as an excellent guide to the opinions of many women of the day. These women formed the Young Ladies' Literary Society in 1813. They met weekly to discuss their views on different subjects, and the answers they agreed on were recorded by the society president (see right).

These questions and answers reveal the public opinions of wealthy women in society at this time. It is interesting to note that the last question, on whether a woman should ever rule a nation, was never answered!

Diaries as evidence

Private diaries are very good sources of information about women's lives in early America. Obviously, the women who kept diaries were literate, which immediately tells historians something about them— very poor women at this time were rarely educated, because they were expected to work from childhood. Women who were able to write would have to be either from very forward-thinking poor families or from families with enough money to educate their girls. Diaries often contain frank opinions about daily life. The diary of Ruth Pease give us a very good idea of what a 23-year-old woman thought was expected of her in early nineteenth-century American society. The words she uses to describe the character to which she aspires paint a picture of the American ideal. Ruth wrote the diary for her own self-improvement, but it is also a very important record for historians. Here is a typical entry of Ruth's resolutions:

"Resolved to endeavor to my utmost to deny whatever is not most agreeable to a good & universally sweet & benevolent quiet, peaceable, contented, easy, compassionate, generous, humble, meek, modest, submissive, obliging, diligent, & industrious, charitable, even, patient, moderate, forgiving sincere temper; and to do at all times what such a temper would lead me to. Examine strictly ever week whether I have done so."

Martha Ballard, a midwife in Massachusetts in the eighteenth century, left a diary of a very different kind. Martha's diary was written as a record of her patients and her duties as a midwife. However, she also includes details of the daily goings-on of Hallowell, Maine, at this time. If we take, for example, the page for March 15-21, 1799, there is a wealth of information about religious, social, and even meteorological events. Remember that these are Martha's words as she wrote them, so some of the spellings may look strange:

"15 Clear and very Pleasant till after noon. my Son Pollard Came here with his Dagt [daughter] Hannah…Saml Trask here, his thumb is Soar [sore]. I advised to a wheat Bran Poultis. Sally washt [washed]…."

EARLY COLONIAL HOME

An early colonial home would have had one large room where everything took place—cooking, eating, and sleeping. The plates on the shelf are made of pewter and would be some of the most expensive things the family owned. The large fire was used for cooking and heating the room. In this reenactment at Plymouth Plantation the woman is playing the part of colonist Tryphosa Tracy and preparing fritters for her family. The fritters will be cooked over the fire on a griddle plate. Her clothes are typical of a woman of her status and age, and the ruff around her neck was very fashionable.

"18th Cloudy and Cold, snowd some at Even…. we are informd Mr Georg Brown has frozen his feet so that part of thim are Come off, a Sad misfortune…."

The perils of frostbite are revealed in this entry, showing just how hard conditions were for colonial people at winter.

"19th Clear and pleast [pleasant]…I was Calld by Capt Littlefield to See his wife who is unwell. I tarried all night at Capt Littlefields."

The difficulties of pregnancy at this time are shown here, as Captain Littlefield calls Martha out to help his wife.

"21st Birth Capt Littlefields 7th Son. Mrs Littlefield had her women this morn and was Safe Deld [delivered] at 10h of a fine Son, her 8th Child…receivd 4/6 in Cash and 5 lb Butter."

This entry gives us important details about family size at this time, because we are told of the birth of Captain Littlefield's seventh son, who was his eighth child. We also learn a little about the nature of childbirth, because Martha describes how Mrs. Littlefield had "her women" with her—they would have been female family and neighbors—to assist with the birth. Some facts about the economy of late eighteenth-century towns are revealed as well, because Martha records that she was paid both in cash and in butter. This single page alone would provide the historian with many facts about life at the time and shows how diaries can be useful in revealing to the historian far more than simply what happened on a single day.

ABOVE: **How the main street of Plymouth Plantation would have looked in 1627, six years after the first Thanksgiving. This is part of a recreation of the original colony and shows visitors what everyday life for the colonists would have been like. The houses are made of wood, with thatched roofs, and each house has its plot of land marked out by a fence. The colonists would have used this land to grow vegetables for themselves and also to keep livestock. The man walking up the street is playing the part of Captain Myles Standish, the military captain of the colony, and the man who led the colonists ashore at Plymouth Rock.**

From this entry we learn that members of the town used Martha as a general doctor, as well as a midwife.

"16th Cloudy and moderate. I have Combd [combed] 14 lb 8 oz flax and knitt Some. Our last Sheep has lambd."

This entry records the daily duties that women like Martha had to carry out, as well as her midwife work. Combing flax and knitting clothes were common chores for colonial women of Martha's status.

"17th Clear. my famely all attended worship Except my Self."

We learn from this that Martha's family all attended church, but for some reason Martha was not with them.

Changing times
The period between the arrival of the first European settlers and the birth of the republic after the Revolutionary War

was one of huge change in America. The nation went from being a fledgling colony to being a free country with its own government. The lives of people living during this period changed dramatically, too. Although women did not achieve anything like equality at this time, their roles did change quite significantly.

When the *Mayflower* first arrived in Provincetown Harbor on November 11, 1620, there were 18 women out of the 102 people on board. Three of the women were pregnant when the *Mayflower* left England, and one gave birth during the journey (and named her son Oceanus). The crew had initially been concerned that the "weak bodies of women" would not survive the voyage, but it turned out to be a man and a boy who died on the journey. The first settlers brought with them strong traditional ideas about the different roles of men and women. The women were put to work right away with their normal chores. In fact, in the

LEFT: **Painting of the *Mayflower*, which carried pilgrims from England to New England in 1620.**

journals of the pilgrims we can see how household chores were responsible for the settler women setting foot in the New World for the first time:

> "Monday the 13 of November...our people went on shore to refresh themselves, and our women to wash, as they had great need."

They went to do the laundry! The list of who was not on board the Mayflower is useful to historians, too. Remember that primary sources carry a lot of information "between the lines" and should not just be taken at face value. Eighteen of the men on the *Mayflower* had decided to take their wives with them on the voyage, but at least five men who traveled had left wives behind in England. Why had they done this? And which decision was the right one? We can only assume that those who left their wives behind did so because they felt that either the journey would be too difficult for them, or that they were needed at home to keep the household (and perhaps business) running. Those who brought their wives with them must have done so either because they could

not bear to be parted from them, or because they thought they would be needed in setting up the colony or to support the men with domestic chores (or perhaps a bit of both). There is evidence that women were thought to be a settling influence on a colony, and that having women present was a sign that the colony was permanent and not just an exploration.

America's first woman

It seems that the Native Americans first encountered by the settlers held similar views about the necessity of wives for men. When the men of the *Mayflower* went out to explore the land, they came across Massasoit, chief of the Wampanoag tribe. The journal of one of the pilgrim men relates the conversations they had with Massasoit:

> "He lighted tobacco for us, and fell to discoursing of England, and of the King's Majesty, marveling that he would live without a wife."

Of course, the *Mayflower* women were by no means the first women to walk on

American soil, and the settler women found they had much to learn from their Native American neighbors, in whose culture women were heavily involved in agriculture. This was something the settlers found strange at first, even cruel. Edward Winslow's journal notes that:

> "The women live a most slavish life, they carry all their burdens, set and dress their corn, gather it in, seek out for much of their food, beat and make ready the corn to eat, and have all household care lying upon them."

But soon the conditions in the colony meant that the settler women, too, would become involved in the manual labor of farming. There is no record of any settler man considering it to be a "slavish life" for his wife. It is possible that some of the women found this experience liberating, if hard work, because it would have been one of the first times they worked side by side with the men, almost on equal terms.

Women and religion

Puritans, who had very strong views about male and female roles, created many of these first colonies. Men were the head of the household and had ownership of their wives and children. Wives were there to support their husbands and do as they said. Women were to be subservient (obedient, or secondary in importance) to men in all ways. One of the earliest sermons preached in the church at Plymouth stated:

> "Let your women keep silence in the churches...that is, they ought so to do."

Quakers, who had more liberal ideas about women in church, established later colonies. They believed that the soul was neither male nor female in the eyes of God, so it made little difference whether you were a man or woman in church.

LEFT: **A row of eighteenth-century houses at Colonial Williamsburg in Virginia, where historians have recreated eighteenth-century life as closely as possible. By studying paintings and records from the time, historians have made the town look very similar to the way it would have over 200 years ago. Reenactments like this help us get a sense of what daily life was like in the period.**

BELOW: **Edenton was the first permanent settlement in North Carolina. Established in the early eighteenth century, it was named in 1722 after Governor Charles Eden. In 1728 it became the capital of the North Carolina colony. This Queen Anne house in Edenton shows how grand and beautiful the houses of wealthy colonials could be.**

Women in the home

At home, however, there was still the expectation that the woman should carry out all the household chores and all the childcare. In fact, throughout this period of American history all domestic duties were the woman's responsibility, no matter if they had been working all day in the fields, in their husband's business, or looking after children. This meant that despite the perception of women as weaker than men, they often had to work longer hours.

Attitudes toward the duties of husbands and wives did soften as time went on. By the eighteenth century men like Benjamin Wadsworth of Boston were recommending a more fair and respectful relationship:

> "The husband's government ought to be gentle and easy, and the wife's obedience ready and cheerful. The husband is called the head of the woman. It belongs to the head to rule and govern. Wives are part of the house and family, and ought to be under the husband's government. Yet his government should not be with rigor, haughtiness, harshness, severity, but with the greatest love, gentleness, kindness, tenderness that may be. Though he governs her, he must not treat her as a servant, but as his own flesh; he must love her as himself...O woman...he is your husband, and the great God commands you to love, honor, and obey him. Yea, though possibly you have greater abilities of mind than he has…he is your husband, God has made him your head, and set him above you, and made it your duty to love and revere him."

It is interesting to note that this source even suggests that women may be more capable than men, but that they should still defer to their husbands, because this was the natural order of things.

Mrs. ABIGAIL BUSH

Portraits can give us much more information about people than simply what they looked like. This eighteenth-century portrait of a wealthy woman shows her wearing the expensive fashions and fabrics of the time. This would show anyone who looked at the portrait that her family was rich enough to be able to afford velvet and silk, and to pay for tailors to make the most up-to-date fashions. Her hair would have taken hours to set in such an elaborate style, which was another sign that Mrs. Bush was rich, since it meant she had enough time on her hands to pay to have her hair dressed. The fact that Mrs. Bush was painted holding a book was meant to show that she was educated. It was usually only wealthy women who could read and write at this time. Poorer women were often not educated, since it was more important for them to work than to go to school.

The miniature portrait may be of her husband.

Revolutionary ideas

The Revolutionary War altered attitudes toward women, but not as radically as you might expect, given the republican aims of liberty and equality. However, while men's attitudes toward women may only have changed a little, it seems that women's attitudes changed a lot. The nation's fight for independence gave many women their first voice in politics, their first taste of business life, and their first opportunity to gather together and discuss world issues. Women may have returned to the home and stove after the war was over, but many did so with knowledge that they could achieve more. Women like Judith Murray, who spoke out for women's equality and education, started to publicly voice what many privately thought:

"The idea of the incapability of women is…totally inadmissible…. I would give my daughters every accomplishment which I thought proper, and to crown all, I would early accustom them to habits of industry, and order…they should be enabled to procure for themselves the necessaries of life, independence should be placed within their grasp, and I would teach them to 'reverence themselves.'"

There was still a very long way to go before women would achieve anything near equality with men, but every great journey must start with a single step. This was certainly a step in the right direction for women.

As you read the primary sources in this book, remember that history never stands still. Every time someone finds an old letter, a diary, or a scribbled note in their attic written by their ancestors, a new opportunity arises to learn more about the past. Each source must be considered relative to the time and place it came from and its limitations respected. These are the real voices of America, and we must listen to what they are saying.

RIGHT: **Some colonial women worked in stores, but usually only if their husband was the owner. This reenactor from Colonial Williamsburg is standing in a replica of an eighteenth-century apothecary shop—the closest thing to a colonial drug store.**

66 In the summer season we planted, tended and harvested our corn, and generally had all of our children with us, but had no master to oversee or drive us. **99**

So said Mary Jemison, who was adopted by the Seneca Indians of the Iroquois Confederacy in 1758. Mary's account of her time with the Seneca tribe is very useful to us because it describes daily life and work. However, it also highlights one of the most difficult things about studying the history of Native Americans. Most of the sources we have were not written by American Indians but by the settlers who came to their land. While they can be useful primary sources, the natural bias of the settlers must be remembered.

Food providers

American Indian society differed from that of the Europeans in many ways. One big difference was the roles that women played in each. As a general rule, in Native American tribes where hunting was the main source of food, the men held the most important roles. But in the tribes that had started to rely more on agriculture and producing their own food, the women held very important positions. Women were responsible for much of the production of the tribe's daily food and for making sure there was enough food to

LEFT: **This nineteenth-century illustration of a woman from the Susquehanna tribe in Delaware shows that Native American women sometimes hunted. The woman is carrying a club and a bow and arrow.**

BELOW: **This nineteenth-century picture shows a family of Plains Indians transporting their possessions on a travois—a triangular frame of wooden poles covered with buffalo rawhide, which could be put up to form a makeshift tepee. Note the woman carrrying her infant on her back in a baby carrier.**

last all year. Food is the most important factor for survival; so, as keepers of the food, women held a lot of power.

Women's roles included gathering nuts, seeds, roots, and fruit from the countryside. They also cultivated crops for the village, which included squash, beans, and corn. Women had to preserve the meat that was caught by the men. They also had to process the other parts of hunted animals. They turned the skins into clothes and other things, and used the bone to make useful tools. Cooking was a major responsibility of the women—in some tribes the cooking was shared between families, the women working together to make the work swifter, easier, and more enjoyable. The role of women as food providers is shown in an account by Edward Winslow of the

creation of the Plymouth Plantation settlement in 1620. When the first settlers arrived and started exploring the new land, they came across local Native American women, who were tending corn crops.

"With much fear they entertained us at first, but seeing our gentle carriage towards them, they took heart and entertained us in the best manner they could, boiling cod and such other things as they had for us."

Winslow's account also shows us that Native American women were able to carry out business deals without the involvement of the men of the tribe. Here, the women who fed the settler men also sell them their animal skins:

"Having well spent the day, we returned to the shallop [boat], almost all the women accompanying us to truck, who sold their coats from their backs, and tied boughs about them, but with great shamefacedness (for indeed they are more modest than some of our English women are)."

Raising children

Native American women were also responsible for rearing and raising children. This was vital for the continuation of the tribe, and so it was a very important role. In the tribes of the Iroquois Confederacy the women's place in society was so important that a child's family tree would be traced back through the mother's family line, not the father's. Iroquois tribes also left the choice of tribal leaders to their women. Although the leaders were men, it was the women who decided whether or not they were capable of doing the job. An eighteenth-century French visitor to the Iroquois lands describes a society in which women are almost more important than men:

ABOVE: **Sketch from 1564 showing women of the Timucua tribe in Florida planting their fields. On the right the men can be seen digging the fields, ready for planting. In most Native American tribes the men prepared the land, and the women planted the seeds.**

RIGHT: **The roles of women and men are illustrated neatly in this painting from 1801. The woman is carrying a basket of food and holding the child's hand, while the man is carrying a bow and axe for hunting.**

"Nothing is more real than this superiority of the women. It is of them that the nation really consists; and it is through them that the nobility of the blood, the genealogical tree [family tree, or ancestry], and the families are perpetuated, all real authority is vested in them. The land, the fields, and their harvest all belong to them…they have charge of the public treasury…the children are their domain."

This is probably an over-simplified view of how Iroquois society worked, but it is an interesting insight into the Iroquois perception of women. They were not viewed as a weaker sex but as having the

WHO WAS SACAGAWEA?

In 1804 two men set out to explore and map the American West, Meriwether Lewis and William Clark. This was dangerous work, since few Americans had ever before visited the land. They would need help on their mission—someone who could help them find food, water, and medicine, communicate with native people for them, and keep them safe if they were heading into danger. This important job was given not to a man but to a young woman named Sacagawea from the Shoshone tribe.

Born in 1788, Sacagawea was only 16 years old when she was offered by her husband, a French Canadian trader, as a guide for Lewis and Clark. She set out on the journey from North Dakota with her newborn child. The exploration was to take them all the way to the Pacific Ocean and back—a trip lasting nearly two years. Lewis and Clark soon discovered that Sacagawea was not only extremely knowledgeable about the local area, and the food and medicine to be found in the fields, she was brave, too. Clark's journals show exactly how much the explorers respected their young Native American guide, without whom their journey would probably have ended in disaster:

"Indeed she has borne with a patience truly admirable, the fatigues of so long a route encumbered with an infant, who is even now, only 19 months old.... In trouble she was full of resources, plucky and determined.... Intelligent, cheerful, tireless, faithful, she inspired us all."

skills to carry out some tasks better than the men of the tribe.

Fur trappers' wives

Native American women often played important roles in the lives of the European settlers, too. You'll read more about one of the most famous Native American women to help a settler in the next chapter, but she was not alone.

Many European fur trappers depended on Native American women for their knowledge of the land and their skills in providing food in, what was to the settlers, a hostile wilderness. The fur trappers often married Native American women. Without these local wives many of them would surely have died. One Native American trapper pointed out:

"In case they meet success with hunting, who is to carry the produce of their labor? Women…also pitch our tents, make and mend our clothing, keep us warm at night; and, in fact, there is no such thing as traveling any considerable distance, or for any length of time, in this country, without their assistance."

Pocahontas

In 1616 the English explorer Captain John Smith wrote to Queen Anne, James I of England's wife, about "a child of twelve or thirteen years of age, whose compassionate pitiful heart gave me much cause to respect her." Who was this brave young girl? Her secret clan name was "Matoaca," but we know her by her nickname, "Pocahontas," or "mischievous child."

Ætatis suæ 21. A. 1616.

Many stories have been written about Pocahontas, starting with records kept by Captain John Smith, and including recent tales such as the popular Disney cartoon movie made in 1995. The stories vary greatly in detail, but all have one thing in common—they cannot be trusted! The one person who could have told us the truth about her life, Pocahontas, left no records, so we have to do the best we can with the information available, being careful to pick out the facts from the fiction.

Pocahontas was born some time around 1595, one of many children of Chief Powhatan, who was chief to more than 25 Native American tribes in what is now Virginia. The first written record about Pocahontas appears in 1607, when English settlers arrived in Jamestown. One of their leaders was Captain John Smith, a brave but boastful man who wrote letters and books about his time in the New World. One day Smith was captured by Powhatan hunters and brought before their chief. After a long

consultation, Smith was made to lie with his head on a stone, while Powhatan's men stood nearby, in Smith's own words,

> "being ready with their clubs, to beat out his brains. Pocahontas the king's dearest daughter...got his head in her arms, and laid her own upon his to save him from death: whereat the Emperor [Powhatan] was contented he should live to make him hatchets, and her bells, beads, and copper."

WHO WAS JOHN SMITH?

John Smith developed a taste for adventure early in his life. In 1596 Smith's father died, so the 16-year-old Smith joined the French forces fighting for Dutch independence from Spain. His next stop was Turkey and then Transylvania, where Captain John Smith—as he was by then known—was captured and sold as a slave. He escaped and returned to England, where he started to plan his trip to the New World. He set sail on December 20, 1606, and finally reached Virginia

four months later. He was soon elected as a leader of Jamestown, and the colony grew under his guidance. Smith loved a good story almost as much as he loved a good adventure, and his many writings of his travels should not be taken as pure fact. He claims to have been saved from death by three different princesses, including Pocahontas. Smith died in 1631 at the age of 51, but his letters and books ensure his story survives—boasts and all.

We only have Smith's word that this event took place, and it may actually have been a ritual of the Powhatan tribe to show mercy. Whatever happened, Captain Smith was allowed to live, and he returned to Jamestown—where he found the colony in the grip of terrible starvation.

Once again Smith credits Pocahontas with life-saving kindness, because she and members of her tribe brought food to the people of Jamestown, keeping them alive.

"Now every once in four or five days, Pocahontas with her attendants, brought him so much provision, that saved many of their lives, that else for all this had starved with hunger."

In the weeks and months that followed, the Powhatan tribe and the Jamestown settlers lived peacefully together. Pocahontas visited the colony often, carrying messages from her father, but in 1613 she was taken hostage by some of the colonists and held for ransom. While being held captive, Pocahontas was educated in the Christian faith and met a tobacco farmer named John Rolfe. Rolfe fell in love with Pocahontas and made a proposal of marriage, as he said,

"For the good of the plantation, the honor of our country, for the glory of God, for mine own salvation...."

Chief Powhatan agreed to the marriage, and on April 5, 1614, Pocahontas became Rebecca Rolfe. This marriage helped strengthen the bond of friendship between the Native Americans and the settlers. In the spring of 1616, when Pocahontas was 22, she and John, and their young son Thomas, traveled to England. Pocahontas was brought before King James I to show the extent of the friendship between His Majesty's settlers in the New World and the native tribes living there. However, on the journey back to Virginia Pocahontas became very ill from what was probably pneumonia or tuberculosis. It was clear she was dying, and in her last moments she comforted her husband, saying

"All must die. 'Tis enough that the child liveth."

Pocahontas was buried where she died, in Gravesend, England, thousands of miles from her homeland.

ABOVE LEFT: **Contemporary painting of Rebecca Rolfe.**

BELOW: **Statue of Pocahontas in the graveyard of St. George's Church, Gravesend, where she is buried.**

SETTLER WOMEN

"One among the rest did kill his wife, powdered her, and had eaten of her before it was known; for which he was executed as he well deserved. Now whether she was better roasted, boiled, or carbonated, I know not; but of such a dish as powdered wife I never heard."

Any new settler woman reading this account of the goings-on in Jamestown must have wondered what she had let herself in for! The first ships to arrive in Virginia in 1607 contained no women. Settling a new land was thought to be men's work and no place for the delicate frame of women. However, before long the settlers started to realize that:

> "The plantation can never flourish till families be planted and the respect of wives and children fix the people on the soil."

Planting with women

The first women arrived in 1608—the wife of Thomas Forrest and her maid, Anne Burras. As the only women in a colony of nearly 200 men, they must have found their new home to be a strange and unfriendly place. By 1609 things were much worse, as Jamestown entered a period known as "the Starving Time." Eighty percent of the settlers died during this terrible winter. We know that Thomas Forrest's wife had a baby during this time, but we don't know if mother and child survived the starvation. Anne

Burras did survive, though—of that we are certain, because she soon became Jamestown's first bride and gave birth to a baby girl called, appropriately, Virginia. Anne Burras had already succeeded in the first task assigned to the women of the New World—to survive long enough to marry and bear children. Lord Bacon, a councilman in Virginia in 1620, made the role of women clear when he declared that:

> "When a plantation grows to strength, then it is time to plant with women as well as with men; that the plantation may spread into generations, and not be ever pieced from without."

"Planting with women" in Jamestown continued in 1619, when the Virginia Company of London ordered that:

> "A fit hundredth might be sent of women, maids young and uncorrupt, to make wives to the inhabitants and by that means to make the men there more settled and less movable...."

This passage shows us something of the English attitude toward women at this time—they were settling influences, who would make the men feel more at home and less likely to give it all up and leave. It was felt that the colony would not be secure until it was full of families, all working together to create new Virginians. Land was offered as an incentive to come to the colony—it was supposed to be just for the male settlers, but it was the men of Jamestown who argued that women were just as deserving of the land as men:

> "Because that in a newe plantation it is not known whether man or woman be the most necessary."

Although the male settlers may have had more muscle power, it seems that it was the female settlers who were the key to making the settlement work.

Reasons for traveling

For some English women the promise of a husband was their main reason for going to the New World. Women who

LEFT: **On July 14, 1776, pioneer Daniel Boone's daughter Jemima and her friends Betsey and Frances Callaway were captured by the Shawnee while rowing across the Kentucky River near Boonesboro. Betsey tried to fend off her attacker with an oar, as this picture shows. The girls were held for two days and nights before being rescued by Boone.**

RIGHT: **This sketch shows the women brought to Jamestown as brides-to-be for the single men. They were known as "tobacco brides" since any who became brides had to be paid for by their new husbands in tobacco.**

BELOW: **Jamestown, situated on the James River, Virginia, as it would have looked in 1615. Jamestown was the first permanent English settlement in America.**

could not find a suitable husband in England were promised that:

> "If they be but civil, and under 50 years of Age, some honest Man or other will purchase them for their Wives."

Other women traveled to the New World as indentured servants. Before the African slave trade began, young English men and women would sign up to be a servant for a term of four to seven years in return for free transportation to the New World. Some women did this to escape an unpleasant home life in England. Some were forced to do it as a punishment for a crime. Others signed up out of a sense of youthful adventure. What they found when they arrived in the New World depended on who they were serving. Some indentured servants were treated well by their masters, while some were treated as slaves. The stories of cruel masters did not often get reported in England: indentured servants were much in demand, and no one wanted to scare them off. A Jamestown settler named John Hammond wrote an account of indentured servitude in Virginia in

1656, trying to deny rumors of hard work and hard masters:

> "The women are not (as is reported) put into the ground to work, but occupy such domestic employments and housewifery as in England, that is dressing victuals [food], right up the house, milking, employed about dairies, washing, sewing, &c. and both men and women have times of recreations, as much or more than in any part of the world besides."

Touching on those women who were sent as convicts, he added:

> "Some wenches that are nastily, beastly and not fit to be so employed are put into the ground, for reason tells us, they must not at charge be transported then maintained for nothing."

While John Hammond's letter should be seen as more of an "advertisement" than a true account of life for indentured servants, it does describe some of the chores of settler women. Unlike their new

A LETTER FROM POOR BETTY

A more truthful account of indentured servitude can be found in a letter from Elizabeth Sprigs to her father in 1756. Elizabeth seems to have been "banished" to America by her father in England. Her life as an indentured servant sounds nothing like that described by John Hammond:

> "What we…suffer here is beyond the probability of you in England to Conceive, let it suffice that I…am toiling almost Day and Night, and very often in the Horses drudgery… and then tied up and whipp'd…scarce any thing but Indian Corn and Salt to eat and that even begrudged… almost naked no shoe nor stockings to wear…what rest we can get is to rap ourselves up in a Blanket and ly upon the Ground, this is the deplorable Condition your poor Betty endures."

Native American neighbors, the English women were not considered equals in this new society. Women could not vote for or hold official positions of power within the colony. A wife's place was at her

ABOVE: **Fear of attacks from neighboring tribes of Native Americans made most colonial women very anti-Indian, sometimes more so than their husbands. In this print from 1704 a Puritan woman in Deerfield, Massachusetts, tries to protect her children against a raid by the Abnaki tribe.**

LEFT: **This illustration of the *Mayflower* passengers arriving at Plymouth Rock shows the typical view of women. They are either shown as mothers of children or as weak and needing help. This scene would not have taken place in real life, since the women had to stay on board ship for four months longer than the men.**

RIGHT: **Life in the colonies was not just hard work, it was dangerous too. Here a pair of gun-toting farm women save their friend from a savage wildcat.**

husband's side, helping him, carrying out all the domestic chores for the family, and ensuring their survival by keeping the food supply constant. After the Virginia colonists realized they could grow and trade tobacco, women found themselves working alongside men in the fields—something they would never have done in England. With so few workers available, there was little time for worrying about whether it was "proper." The hard work and survival abilities of many of the settler women made them much admired by their husbands and fellow colonists. This is not to say that new ideals of equality were achieved in the New World colonies, but that necessity made the lines between the role of men and women more blurred than they would ever have been back home in England.

A Woman rescued from the Jaws of a Catamount.

COURTSHIP AND MARRIAGE

66 The happiness of your life now depends on the continuing to please a single person. To this all other objects must be secondary, even your love for me. **99**

Thomas Jefferson's instructions to his daughter Martha in 1790 reveal the duties expected of a bride in early America. Marriage was seen as almost a necessity for women at this time. It was a mixed blessing, however. Once married, a woman immediately lost all her legal rights. This was a system called coverture. It meant:

- all property was automatically owned by the husband even if it had originally belonged to the wife;
- the wife could not buy or sell anything, or sign a contract, without her husband's permission;
- the husband had complete control over any children from the marriage.

One of the rights of a husband was:

> "The care and power...for the disposing of Children in Marriage."

This meant that it was the father who had the final say over whether or not a marriage took place.

Colonial courtship

Courtship was not usually a romantic period of "dating" between a young couple. It was more like a formal request to a young woman's father by a young man. If the young woman's father was a reasonable man, he might let his daughter have a say in the match. This was the case for Hannah Taylor in 1794. When Elihu Hoyt wrote to Hannah's

24

uncle (her legal guardian) requesting her hand in marriage, Hannah's uncle wrote back giving his blessing, but saying:

> "I do not hold myself at Liberty, to controul her, in her Inclinations, in Regard to that which more nearly concerns herself, than any other Person."

He left the final say to Hannah, deciding it was not his place to make such a decision for her. True love did exist in courtship and marriage, of course. This extract of a letter from James McHenry to John Caldwell shows the adoration James had for John's sister Margaret:

> "If I could not be happy with her I could be happy with no other woman. There is a charm in her…more pleasing than even beauty itself…I now see before me a sure prospect of rest, and of uncommon felicity [happiness] in the tenderest connection….When you are as much in love as I am, and are loved in your turn, you will find a pleasure in writing to your mistress and in receiving from her a letter."

James's courting paid off, and the two were married in January 1784, when Margaret was 22. The age at which a woman was married depended on her family's status, and where they lived in America. In the South many women had to wait until their indentured servitude was over before they could marry. This meant they were often in their late twenties before their wedding day. Puritan women living in seventeenth- and eighteenth-century New England married the youngest—as young as midteens, though the normal age for marriage in New England was nearer the early twenties.

Generally, the wealthier the family, the younger their children married. The transformation from child to wife could be a difficult and shocking one for a girl in her teens, especially because motherhood was expected to come shortly afterward. It could also be a difficult change for women who married later and had experienced independent life for many years.

SAMUEL ADAMS'S ADVICE ON MARRIAGE

This letter of November 22, 1780, from Samuel Adams to Thomas Wells (who was engaged to Samuel's daughter, Hannah) emphasizes the thought that had to go into the union from both sides to ensure a happy marriage:

> "The Marriage State was designed to complete the Sum of human Happiness in this life, It some times proves otherwise. But this is owing to the Parties themselves, who either rush into it without due Consideration, or fail in…their Conduct towards each other afterwards. It requires Judgment on both Sides…for though it is acknowledged, that the Superiority is & ought to be in the Man, yet as the Management of a Family in many Instances necessarily devolves on the Woman, it is difficult always to determine the Line between the Authority of the one & the Subordination of the other."

CHILDBIRTH

> **66 About 2 in ye morning Widow Newton rouses me with the News of a Safe deliverance & ye birth of a Son of extraordinary Size and Fatness.... 99**

It was with these words that Eben-ezer Parkman recorded the birth of his son Elias in mideighteenth-century Massachusetts. It is no surprise that Ebenezer was sleeping while his wife was in the next room giving birth. Childbirth was no place for a man. Most women were helped by a number of female friends and relatives during their labor. In early colonial America midwives were usually older women who had no formal training but a lot of experience. Towns considered themselves very lucky to have a midwife, and many tried to attract midwives with promises of free housing or large payments. The work of midwives is explained well in one of the bestselling books of the mideighteenth century. *Aristotle's Complete Masterpiece* contained advice to midwives on how to attend pregnant women and advice for mothers-to-be on how to look after themselves during pregnancy and childbirth (see box).

Native American childbirth

Native American women took a very different view of labor—often taking themselves away from the village into the

THE MIDWIFE'S HANDBOOK

Aristotle's Complete Masterpiece was published in many forms and could contain up to four parts. The first, his *Complete Masterpiece*, is subtitled "Displaying the Secrets of Nature in the Generation of Man." Additions include: *Family Physician*—"approved Remedies for the several Distempers incident to the human body"; *Experienced Midwife*: "absolutely necessary for Surgeons, Midwives, Nurses, and Child-bearing Women"; *Book of Problems*: which contains "various Questions and Answers, relative to the State of Man's Body" and his *Last Legacy*, which looked at the "Secrets of Nature, respecting the Generation of Man."

The sort of advice covered is shown in this example:

"When the time of birth draws near, the woman must be sure to send for a skilful midwife, and that rather too soon than too late….When everything is thus ready, and when the woman feels the pains coming on, if the weather be not cold, she should walk about the room, rest on the bed occasionally, waiting for the breaking of the waters….If she be very weak she may take some mild cordial [medicinal drink] to give her strength, if her pain will permit her; and if the labor be tedious, she may be revived with chicken or mutton broth, or she may take a poached egg; but she must be very careful not to eat to excess…two women must hold her shoulders…and let one stroke or press the upper part of her stomach gently and by degrees. The woman herself must not be nervous or downhearted, but courageous, and forcing herself by straining and holding her breath….When the head appears, the midwife must hold it gently between her hands, and draw the child, whenever the woman's pains are upon her, but at no other times; slipping her forefingers under its armpits by degrees, and not using a rough hand in drawing it out, lest the tender infant might become deformed by such means."

LEFT: **This is the birth and baptismal certificate for Catharina Heilman, who was born in 1777 in Lebanon Township, Lancaster County. This area of Pennsylvania was settled by German Jews at this time, which is why the certificate is in German. Also written on the certificate is a blessing, to wish the child well through its life.**

BELOW: **This unusual scene of a colonial childbirth shows a man attending the pregnant woman—it is very likely that he is her husband. The three female attendants are probably family or friends and possibly a midwife. With no medical facilities nearby, families just had to hope that nothing went wrong.**

woods, with only one or two attendants. In some tribes labor was a solitary business, with women giving birth alone.

There was no such thing as pain relief in childbirth at this time. In fact, the pain of labor was seen as something a woman simply must bear. It was considered a punishment for the sin of Eve, when she ate the apple in the Garden of Eden. Women were supposed to suffer with as little fuss as possible, and were urged to

> "Keep quiet those dreadful groans and cries which do so much discourage their friends and relations that are near them."

In Native American societies it was believed that if a woman showed any pain

in labor, her children would become cowards.

Risks and misfortunes

Pregnancy and childbirth were risky businesses, and neither was fully understood at this time, not even by midwives and doctors. For instance, it was believed that for a woman to even just lay eyes on something unpleasant during pregnancy would cause damage to her child. *Aristotle's Complete Masterpiece* contains cautionary tales of such misfortune:

> "Many women, in being with child, on seeing a hare cross the road in front of them, will, through the force of imagination, bring forth a child with a hairy lip. Some children are

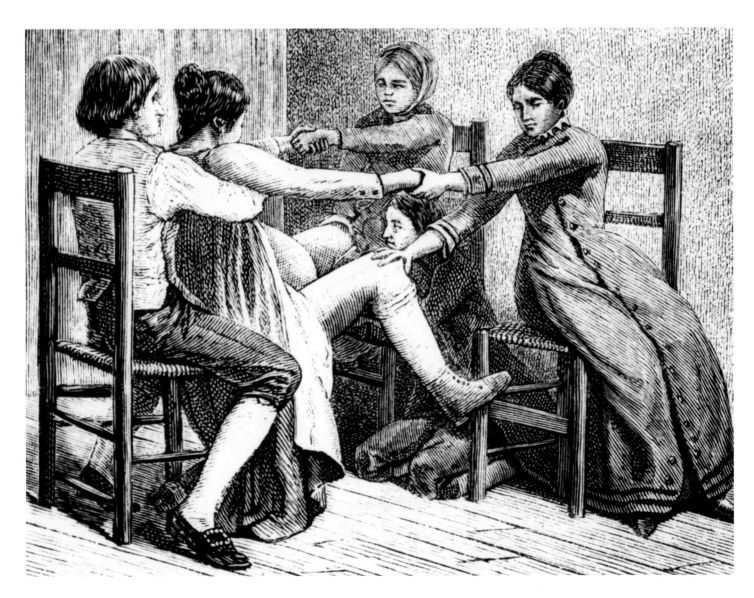

MAN-MIDWIFERY—
A GOOD IDEA OR A CRIME AGAINST NATURE?

Up to the end of the eighteenth century it would have been considered obscene for a man to carry out a midwife's tasks. The very name midwife shows that it was considered to be the work of women for women. With the end of the century came a change in thought. Male doctors and physicians started to assist at births. This stirred huge controversy in Britain and America—not only was it considered improper for a man to attend a woman in this way, it was thought that men relied too much on the use of surgical instruments, which could harm the baby. John Maubray, a supporter of men as midwives, wrote in 1724:

"Men...being better versed in Anatomy, better acquainted with Physical Helps, and commonly endued with greater presence of Mind, have been always found...to give

quicker Relief in cases if difficult or preternatural births, than common midwives generally understand."

In opposition to this view was Sarah Stone, who wrote *A Complete Practice of Midwifery* in 1737. In Sarah's opinion:

"There are many sufferers, both mothers and children; yea, infants have been born alive, with their brains working out of their heads, occasioned by the too common use of instruments."

This image from the time shows the forceps, blunt hook, and levers of the man-midwife, and the warm hands and gentle methods of the female midwife. Male midwives gradually grew in popularity over this period, especially among wealthy people, who saw them as a way of following fashion and displaying wealth.

born with flat noses and wry mouths, great blubber lips and ill-shaped bodies; which must be ascribed to the imagination of the mother, who has cast her eyes and mind upon some ill-shaped creature."

In mortal fear

The haunting image of death was also closely associated with childbirth. One in eight women died in childbirth, and the whole business was not greeted with the joy and happiness that it is today. Instead, it was approached with the dread of what could go wrong. With no skilled surgeons and modern medicines to help out, women often expected the worst. The seventeenth-century poet Anne Bradstreet wrote a poem called *Before the Birth of One of Her Children*, which was almost a goodbye to her husband in case she died while giving birth:

> How soon, my Dear, death may my
> steps attend.
> How soon't may be thy lot to lose thy
> friend,

The lines reveal exactly how much Anne feared the worst from childbirth.

Populating the New World

Although it was dangerous, child rearing was considered to be a very important role for women, and large families were normal. Women could expect to be pregnant very soon after marriage (some were even pregnant before) and then to have a child every two or so years until they became infertile or they died. Eight or ten children were not unusual, and some families contained many more. In this way the settlers of the New World hoped to quickly populate the land with Americans to ensure their survival. An essay written by Benjamin Franklin in 1751 illustrated the impact of large families on colonizing the New World:

> "If in Europe they have but 4 Births
> to a Marriage (many of their
> Marriages being late) we may here
> reckon 8, of which if one half grow
> up, and Marriages are made,
> reckoning one with another at 20
> Years of Age, our People must at least
> be doubled every 20 Years."

Large families were not only important to increase the population. Children were a vital workforce on a family farm and often the providers of money in their parents' old age. With at least a quarter of children dying in infancy, it was important to have as many children as possible so that enough would live to working age. When a woman safely delivered a child, it was an occasion for celebration. There were often feasts at the bedside of the mother shortly after the child was born. The diary of Samuel Sewall, a judge in colonial Boston, records that after his wife delivered their twelfth child, he found the female attendants by her bedside celebrating with:

> "Ros Beef and minc'd Pyes, good
> Cheese and Tarts."

This menu, added to the "groaning ale," a potent beer for the pregnant mother to drink during labor, paints a very different picture from childbirth today.

BELOW: **A Native American woman in labor squats with her back against a tree as another woman kneels before her blowing smoke from a pipe between her legs.**

BELOW LEFT: **Seventeenth-century woodcut of a midwife assisting in a delivery, around 1621.**

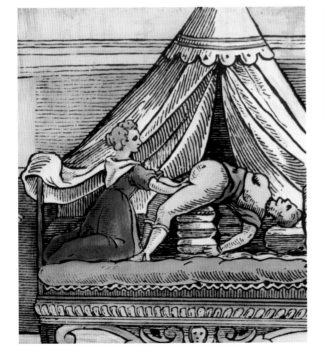

> **"When I had but one Child my hands were tied, but now I am tied hand and foot (how I shall get along when I have got half a dozen or 10 children I can't devise)."**

This is an entry from the journal of Esther Edwards Burr after the birth of her second child, Aaron, in 1756. Sadly, Esther was unable to find out how she would cope with more children, because she and her husband died of smallpox when Aaron was only two. Esther's words do show how many women feared they would not be able to cope with the task of bringing up a large family. So how did women cope? The answer is, with help.

Colonial women were confined to the house for about 10 months after labor—they had to be near their children for breastfeeding, and it was thought that new mothers should not venture far until about 10 to 12 months. As with childbirth, female friends and relatives rallied round and helped the new mother, both in her daily chores and with the baby. It was common for many women to be pregnant or rearing children at the same time in the new colonies, so women sometimes even helped to wet-nurse each other's children.

What's in a name
A child would be named in a baptism service about two or three days after birth. It was believed that the name of the child would be an important factor in how it grew up, so children were often named after well-respected members of the family or community. Early Puritan names reflected the desire of the early settlers to have children that were morally correct and well behaved. Girls' names like "Thankful," "Remembrance," and "Silence" were not unheard of. More extreme names have been recorded for Puritan boys, including "Fear," "Experience," and even "Fight-the-good-fight-of-faith" and "Killsin." Baptism was not only important for giving the new child a name, it was also seen as the start of their salvation. Christians in early America believed that all children were born in a natural state of sin. It was the responsibility of the parents to cleanse their children of this sin. Cotton Mather, the seventeenth-century New England preacher, explained the natural state of sin found in children:

> "Don't you know, That your Children, are the Children of Death, and the Children of Hell, and the

ABOVE: **This portrait of Sir William Pepperrell and his family in 1778 shows that children were really the mother's domain. The father looks at his children almost as if they are playthings for his amusement.**

BELOW: **Native American women had a clever way of keeping their children from harm. This sketch from 1703 shows how the baby would be hung from a tree in a special bag so the mother could work without worrying about her child.**

attaché à une

Children of Wrath, by Nature….You must know, Parents, that your Children are by your means Born under the dreadful Wrath of God."

It was the responsibility of parents to save their children from sin by teaching them to be good and godly. This meant that children were often raised in a serious environment rather than in fun and play. The Reverend John Robinson, a minister at Plymouth, advised a heavy hand to raise a godly child:

"Surely there is in all children…a stubbornness and stoutness of mind arising from natural pride which must first be in the first place broken and beaten down."

Anne Bradstreet, the poet, offered a different view of how children should be raised:

"Diverse children have their different natures; some are like flesh which nothing but salt will keep from putrefaction; some again like tender fruits that are best preserved with sugar: those parents are wise that can fit their nurture according to their Nature."

A dangerous time

Danger lurked everywhere for infants in early America—fires, open wells, dirt, and disease—and the infant mortality rate was high in the new colonies. In the diaries of Samuel Sewall we can glimpse what terrible misfortunes happened to some of the children of seventeenth-century New England—killed by being dragged off by a galloping horse, drowning in local rivers, being burned to death from cook-pots in the home, even being accidentally shot by hunters. It's a wonder anyone survived to adulthood!

BELOW: **Detail from "The First Thanksgiving" by Jennie Augusta Brownscombe showing a colonial mother rocking her baby to sleep in a wooden crib.**

> **" A lady who has been seen as a sloven or slut [untidy in appearance] in the morning will never efface the impression she has made, with all dress and pageantry she can afterwards involve herself in....I hope therefore, the moment you rise from bed, your first work will be to dress yourself in such style as that you may be seen by any gentleman without his being able to discover a pin amiss. "**

Thomas Jefferson's letter to his daughter illustrates that the home life of a well-to-do lady of the eighteenth century started with the way she looked. For a woman of money, like Jefferson's daughter, home life was a routine of ladylike pursuits and improving activities. Little work would have been done by such women, though they would have been responsible for overseeing the work of servants or slaves. Wealthy women in such households were managers, as well as trophies for husbands to display. It was vital that a wealthy woman take care of her appearance so that she would do nothing to hurt her husband's reputation. (Note that Jefferson describes his daughter's dressing herself as "work.")

The perfect hostess

Wealthy women were expected to provide the finishing touches to their homes, to make them appear gracious and welcoming, and most importantly, to be good hosts. Hospitality was a very important sign of wealth and breeding, and women were expected to become perfect hostesses at the drop of a hat. Guests did not always announce when they planned to visit and could often stay for a number of days. If a hostess failed to meet their every need with food and drink and comfortable beds, her family would become objects of gossip and scorn in the neighborhood. It was not just wealthy women with servants who were expected to care for guests in this way. Eliza Haywood of Raleigh was forced to prepare business dinners for her husband and as many as 30 of his

To the Right Honorable Randal William McDonnell, EARL of ANTRIM, VISCOUNT DUNLUCE, BARON of ANTRIM, LORD LIEUTENANT of the COUNTY of ANTRIM, and KNIGHT of the Most Honorable Military Order of the BATH, This Plate representing the common Method of Beetling, Scutching and Hackling the Flax is gratefully Inscribed by his Lordships grateful humble Servant W. HINCKS.

colleagues night after night. Eliza had recently given birth to her fourth child, and she writes to her mother of being:

"Almost worn out and Broke down, with Fatigue and want of rest."

Another hostess at the same time paints a picture of acting out of duty, despite her feelings for her guests, who were:

"Utterly odious [hated] to me, the very last people in the county with whom I will be familiar, and yet I am forced to 'make a dinner' for their dainty palates [tastes], with all the labor and turmoil which a young housekeeper must have on such occasions, and deck my face with

smiles of welcome, while in my heart I would rather see them on their way…to the S.E. corner of h—l [hell]."

Dirty and distressed

In stark contrast to the elegant picture Jefferson paints of home life for his daughters, the July 7, 1769, journal entry of Mary Cooper, a colonial housewife, reads:

"Hot as yesterday. I am dirty and distressed, almost weared to death. Dear Lord, deliver me."

Mary lived on Long Island and married at the tender age of 14. She first became a mother at the age of 20 and had six children, all of whom died before she

ABOVE: **A colonial wife tends a cooking pot on her kitchen fire. A broom at left shows her cleaning chores. Various instruments for food preparation can be seen hanging on the wall.**

BELOW LEFT: **Here a colonial family works together to process flax. Everyone was expected to play their part, the women and children just as much as the men.**

ABOVE: **This scene of a town pump shows only women gathering water. Collecting water was seen as a woman's job, even though it was physically demanding. Some women did not live near a pump and so had to rely on rivers and springs for their water supply.**

LEFT: **An Iroquois woman pounding corn with a pestle and log mortar, her child hanging safely nearby. The cradle was a board about two feet long, with a projecting bow. It and the top edge of the board were often carved. Near the bottom was a foot support. The baby was bound to the board with red or blue cloth decorated with beads or moose hair, and a blanket or netting could be drawn over the bow to protect the baby's face. A strap secured the cradle behind the mother's shoulders.**

did. In the entry July 13, 1769, Mary writes:

"This day is forty years since I left my father's house and come here, and here have I seene little else but harde labour and sorrow, crosses of every kind. I think in every respect the state of my affairs is more then forty times worse then when I came here first, except that I am near the desired haven. A fine clear cool day. I am un well."

It is not surprising that Mary's life was so exhausting. Her journal records her household chores, which included: cleaning; cooking, preserving, and salting meat; making sausages; picking fruit; preserving fruit as jams; drying apples and cherries; pickling fruits and vegetables; washing and ironing clothes; baking bread and pies; making wine and ale; making soap and candles; beekeeping; processing flax; spinning; and sewing.

These jobs would have been familiar to any woman of average wealth at this time. With no washing machines or vacuum cleaners, even the most routine chores could be backbreaking. Just doing the family's laundry could take three or four days. Add to this the responsibility for keeping the house stocked with water (all gathered from a well or spring, which could be a long walk away) and for keeping the fires burning. There would have been little opportunity for rest.

The fire was the heart of the colonial house, and it was the woman's role to ensure it did not go out. A dead fire meant no cooking, no warm water for washing, no candle making, and no heat. Most fires consumed an average of about 50 pounds of wood per day, and every pound had to be carried by the woman of the house. She had to make sure the fire was well fed and hot enough for whatever was needed of it.

Stitching and sewing

Making clothing was a crucial role of women in the home. While wealthy women, like Jefferson's daughters, could afford to pay someone else to make their clothes, the average family relied on the women to make everything they wore. This meant starting off with the raw materials—the cotton, flax, or wool—that were first spun into yarn and then woven into cloth. Then the cloth would be cut and stitched to make anything from a simple bonnet to a special party dress. Stores sold cloth, but it made more sense for women to make their own. It was cheaper, and they could sell any extra they didn't need. In the eighteenth century mills started to become more common, and women could buy cloth instead of always having to make it. Clothes were still usually made at home, however, as this letter of February 11, 1785, noted. Cynthia Williams of Deerfield, Massachusetts, writes to her brother, apologizing that:

"We can not help you to any breeches [pants] at present, have been so unlucky as to have ye Mill break while our cloth was in, and it is not done, our Boys are almost naked."

Women were expected to be able to spin, weave, and make clothes—something they would have learned from their mother. In fact, most household tasks would have been learned from a woman's mother, grandmother, or other female family member. These skills were essential for succeeding in life—a man was likely to choose a wife based on her ability to look after him, so a woman had to learn how to run a household from an early age. The colonial farmer and writer J. Hector St. John de Crevecoeur told his wife that:

"Hadst thee never employed thyself in thy father's house to learn and to practice the many branches of house-keeping that thy parents were famous for, thee wouldst have made but a sorry wife for an American farmer; thee never shouldst have been mine. I married thee not for what thee hadst, but for what thee knewest."

BELOW: **Cooking was a key responsibility for women at this time, and food preparation probably took up much of their time. Meals would be cooked for the extended family, and often a little had to go a very long way.**

"Sometimes I delight in inventing and executing machines, which simplify my wife's labor."

The colonial farmer and writer J. Hector St. John de Crevecoeur doesn't tell us what his wife's labors were, or whether his machines helped her. But we can assume that he means housework. As

we saw before, women in early colonial America spent almost all their time engaged in household work. This did not simply involve cooking and cleaning but also weaving cloth, making clothes, preserving meat, spinning yarn, gathering water, grinding corn, making soap and candles, and countless other tasks that ensured the family's survival. All this was done in addition to raising large families, being almost constantly in a state of pregnancy or nursing a child, and sometimes both. A woman's work during this period of history was every bit as hard as a man's, even though it was seen as being simply her domestic role in life.

For wealthier women the list of chores was the same, but they had servants and, later, slaves to help them with their workload.

Early businesswomen

There were women, however, who entered into a different type of work— the business world. Single women sometimes got jobs as seamstresses, kept boarding houses, or taught in small schools. Women who lost their husbands but had no sons old enough to take over their father's business often ran the business themselves. Thus there were cases of women printers, blacksmiths, shopkeepers, and other professions in colonial society. Women also supported their husbands in their work. Crevecouer records the tale of one such woman who was so good at running her husband's affairs that she built up his fortune without any help from him. It is interesting to note that Crevecouer regards the woman with respect and admiration, suggesting he didn't find it unusual for a woman to get involved in her husband's business:

"The richest person now in the island owes all his present prosperity and success to the ingenuity of his wife…for while he was performing his first cruises, she traded with pins and needles, and kept a school. Afterward she purchased more considerable articles, which she sold with so much judgement, that she laid the foundation of a system of business, that she has ever since prosecuted with equal dexterity and success. She wrote to London, formed connections, and, in short, became the only ostensible instrument [visible means of support] of that house, both at home and abroad.…To this dexterity [skill] in managing the husband's business whilst he is absent, the Nantucket wives unite a great deal of industry. They spin, or cause to be spun in their houses, abundance of wool and flax; and would be for ever disgraced and looked upon as idlers if all the family were not clad in good, neat, and sufficient homespun cloth."

War and manufacturing

Two key events changed the role of working women and saw them join the labor force instead of working from home: war and the start of manufacturing. The French and Indian War (in Europe the conflict was known as the Seven Years War) started in 1756, and many men left their work to go and fight. Women took over their husband's role to keep their business afloat. Suddenly, in towns that were used to only men being in business, there were women running the local stores, the blacksmith's forge, butcher shop, and everywhere else that had previously been a male territory. Many men died in the war, so what had started as a temporary solution turned into a permanent career for some women.

When Europeans first colonized America, all goods were made to order by hand in small numbers. But gradually, with more industrial advancements, it became easier to set up factories to produce goods quickly on a large scale. These factories needed one thing to make sure they could function—workers. Suddenly there was a need for many pairs of hands to operate machines and carry out

ABOVE LEFT: **An American colonial-era woman reads a book as she spins yarn on a spinning wheel, 1700s.**

LEFT: **Before the emergence of factories in the eighteenth century most manufacturing was done at home on a small scale. Here a group of women work together at home, spinning in a variety of different ways.**

RIGHT: **Two women using old-fashioned spinning wheels, about 1800.**

ELIZABETH MURRAY: BUSINESSWOMAN

Elizabeth was a remarkable woman when it came to the world of business. Born in Scotland in 1726, she moved by herself to Boston in 1748, aged 22. With help from her brother James Elizabeth established a store in Boston, selling the sorts of luxury items that colonial women wanted to buy. In addition to Elizabeth's successful store she also set up a needlework school and ran a boarding house. This advertisement from a Boston newspaper of 1753 touts Elizabeth's roles as teacher, boarding house landlady, and shopkeeper:

"ELIZABETH MURRAY TEACHES Dresden, and other kinds of Needle Works, likewise accommodates young Ladies with Board, and half Board, at a reasonable Price; sells flowered and clear Lawns, Cambricks, Muslins, Gauze, newest Fashion Caps, Ruffles, Tippits, Stomachers, Solitairs, Necklaces, Ear Rings, Ivory, Ebony and Bone Stick Fans, Women's Shoes, Stockings, Gloves and Mittens, Canvas, Crewils, Floss, Flower-ing and Nuns Threads, Needles, Pins and Tapes, with sundry other Articles."

Elizabeth even made her three husbands sign prenuptial agreements so that her property was not automatically given to them under the legal system of coverture. Elizabeth Murray was an unusual woman of her time and admitted that "I have acted many roles in life." However, she demonstrated the growing interest and influence that women had in the business world, something also helped by the start of the manufacturing industry.

manufacturing tasks. At a time when most men were busy with their own businesses, farming, or away as soldiers, women became an obvious choice for these positions. In 1791 the first secretary of the Treasury, Alexander Hamilton, wrote a *Report on Manufactures*, in which he noted:

"There are circumstances...that materially diminish every where the effect of a scarcity of hands. These circumstances are—the great use which can be made of women and children...."

The British blockades set up during the Revolutionary War meant there were serious shortages of most manufactured items. It was more crucial than ever for America to make its own goods, and this placed more demands

on the manufacturing industries. Women became an essential workforce in cotton mills, iron mills, paper mills, and countless other factories. They were cheaper to hire than men and just as hard working. Life for these women was not easy because they worked long hours in what could be very unpleasant conditions. They then had to return home and carry out all the domestic chores expected of them, as well as caring for their families. However, this work provided women with a wage at a time when they may have been struggling alone to bring money into the family. Some women were made widows by the war and faced extreme poverty if they could not find some way of supporting themselves. With factory work

Although they may not have known it, women who worked outside the home during this period were forging an important path for the future. They proved that women could be as successful as men in the business and labor world.

LEFT: **This illustration of weaving and spinning come from the book *Orbis Pictus* ("The world in pictures") by Johannes Amos Comenius. Published in 1657, it is considered the first children's book. The woman on the right is carding wool, which will then be spun into twine by her children at the wheel. The twine would then be made into cloth by the husband at the loom.**

BELOW: **About 1610 a Virginia family works together in spinning and processing cotton.**

"Poor women and children can earn from 20 to 40 cents per day in moating cotton."

Printing was one industry that benefited greatly from the input of women during this period. Two women in particular made names for themselves in printing.

The first was Anne Catherine Hoof Green. Anne was born in the Netherlands in about 1720 and came to America as a child. Anne married Jonas Green, a Philadelphia printer, in 1738, and the couple moved to Annapolis. In 1767 tragedy struck when Jonas died. Having already learned the trade by watching and helping her husband, Anne chose to continue her husband's printing business, and in 1768 she was formally recognized as being a printer herself.

The *Maryland Gazette* was the most well-read publication from Anne's printing business, and it was an important source of news during the Revolutionary War. Anne died on March 23, 1775, and the *Maryland Gazette* was her lasting legacy.

At the same time as Anne was printing in Annapolis, Mary Katherine Goddard was gaining fame for printing elsewhere in Maryland. Mary was born in Connecticut in 1738; and when her father died in 1762, Mary moved with her mother to Rhode Island to help her brother William in his printing business. Mary learned the trade quickly, and by 1775 she was listed in the *Maryland Journal* as its editor and publisher. Mary's most famous printing job came in 1777, when she printed the Declaration of Independence, which listed all the signers for the first time.

“We are acquainted, that the Reason of the Woman's Creation was the supply of Man's Need and Comfort.... And tho' if the Wife finds her Husband not so Kind as she would Rationally expect, she ought to...bear it as a Consequent of Sin.”

These words formed part of a sermon delivered on July 27, 1703, by the Puritan minister Samuel Willard. His words may seem shocking to us, because they are so obviously sexist (suggesting that women are inferior to men). However, Reverend Willard was only repeating a belief that was key to the Puritan faith—that men were naturally superior, and that women were constant reminders of the sin of Eve in the Garden of Eden.

Puritans

With this in mind it would be easy to assume that women were anti-Puritan. However, early New England was full of Puritan women, living by the rules of their religion and openly accepting their inferiority. In fact, in seventeenth-century New England women outnumbered men in church attendance, something preacher Cotton Mather referred to in 1692 when he said there were “far more godly women” than men. Religion was a common reason for coming to the New World in the first place. Most of the first shiploads of people who arrived at Plymouth after the *Mayflower* were Puritans escaping from religious persecution in England. Other Christians in the New World were sent by their own country to populate the world with god-fearing people. The settlers in Virginia, sent by King James of England, were followers of the Church of England.

Although these varied forms of Christianity differed in some beliefs and practices, they all viewed women as lower than men and said that their presence in church should be seen but not heard. Religion was an important help in the lives of colonial women. At a time when one in eight births could result in the death of the mother, it was important to have faith and believe in an afterlife. All the major life events for a

LEFT: **This woodcut shows a couple from Salzburg who settled in the New World to find religious tolerance.**

FAR LEFT: Hannah Adams (1755–1831) was a noted American historian specializing in the field of religion. In 1784 she wrote *An Alphabetical Compendium of the Various Sects Which Have Appeared from the Beginning of the Christian Era to the Present Day*, which tried to describe the many religions at that time without using words that judged them as good or bad, something no one had attempted before then.

LEFT: Elizabeth Ann Bayley Seton (1774–1821) in a 1797 painting. Elizabeth was the founder and first superior of the Sisters of Charity, a group of religious women who worked in education and with the poor and needy. The Sisters of Charity are still active today and have many different ministries of women helping people all over the world. Elizabeth was canonized as the first American-born saint in 1975.

ANNE BRADSTREET

A devout Puritan living in Massachusetts in the seventeenth century, Anne became famous as the first published poet of the American colonies, and religion was a topic she wrote about a lot. The depth of her religious belief is shown in a poem she wrote after her house burned down in 1666. Even after such a tragic event Anne finds reason to thank God:

"And to my God my heart did cry
To strengthen me in my distress
And not to leave me succorless...
And when I could no longer look,
I blest His name that gave and took,
That laid my goods now in the dust.
Yea, so it was, and so 'twas just.
It was His own, it was not mine,
Far be it that I should repine;
...Raise up thy thoughts above the sky
That dunghill mists away may fly.

Thou hast an house on high erect,
Framed by that mighty Architect...
There's wealth enough, I need no more,
Farewell my pelf, farewell my store,
The world no longer let me love,
My hope and treasure lies above."

There is evidence, however, that Anne was uncomfortable with the Puritan idea of men being superior. In the introduction to a book of her poems called *The Tenth Muse*, published in 1650, Anne shows anger toward those who tell her that a woman should spend her time sewing rather than writing poetry:

"I am obnoxious to each carping tongue,
 Who sayes, my hand a needle better fits,
 A Poets Pen, all scorne, I should thus
     wrong;
For such despight they cast on female
     wits:"

woman—baptism, marriage, childbirth—were religious events, and the belief in God and an afterlife must have made the inevitable pain of losing a child (or many) easier for women to bear. Women swore themselves firmly to follow their God, and it is highly unlikely that any woman at this time would have declared herself an atheist.

The diary of Ruth Pease, born in 1789, shows the importance placed on living a religious life. Ruth's resolutions include many religious promises:

"Resolved to study the scriptures frequently, and to strive to my utmost, every week to make advances in human and divine knowledge....Resolved frequently to renew the dedication of myself to God which was made at my baptism....Resolved never hence forward till I die to act as if I were my own but entirely and altogether Gods."

ANNE HUTCHINSON

Anne Hutchinson was born in Lincolnshire, England, in July 1591 and moved to America with her husband Will and their 15 children in 1634. Anne and her family were Puritans and had moved to New England to find freedom to practice their religion in the way they thought best. Anne formed a woman's club in her town and encouraged other local women to come along to discuss the Bible, to pray, and to talk about the sermons that they had heard. This sort of meeting was very unusual at the time, and many of the men in the town did not approve. They felt Anne was becoming too loud and confident in her views, and that as a woman she should be more subservient and serve God in the way she was told to at church. Anne was banished from her community, and in 1643 she and five of her children were attacked and killed by Mahicans in East Chester, New York. Many saw this tragedy as God's final judgment on Anne.

Quaker women

In the middle colonies—New York, New Jersey, Pennsylvania, and Delaware—the sheer number of different religious communities living side by side created an environment where women could play a stronger role in religion than the Puritan faith allowed. Anglicans, Jews, Lutherans, Roman Catholics, and Baptists had all settled in the same area, and a mood of religious tolerance existed there out of necessity. It was here that the Quakers settled in the late seventeenth century to practice their religion in a land free from the strict rules of the Puritans.

Quakers believed that the soul could not be male or female—this meant that all souls were equal no matter what gender. Quaker men were still seen as the head of the household, but Quaker women were allowed to speak at religious meetings—a freedom denied by the Puritans. Women also had their own meeting houses for religious business. William Penn, who founded Pennsylvania for the Quaker faith, explained why women-only meetings were useful for both women and for the Quaker Church in a pamphlet called *Just Measures*, published in 1692:

"But why Women apart, say you? We think for a very Good Reason…. Women, whose Bashfulness will not permit them to say, or do much as to Church Affairs before the Men, when by themselves, may exercise their Gifts, of Wisdom and Understanding, in a discreet Care for their own Sex."

Native American religions

Quaker societies were not only open-minded in their views toward women, they also encouraged tolerance of other cultures. The Quakers were the first group to speak out against slavery. They also made an agreement to live in peace with their Native American neighbors. Other religions tried to force themselves onto Native American culture. Within the Catholic faith women often served their religion by becoming nuns. These nuns traveled to the New World as missionaries to try to convert the Native Americans to the Catholic faith.

Native Americans had many different religions, varying from tribe to tribe. They all had common convictions, however, in that they all believed in some kind of creator, who made them, and an afterlife. The Native American religions served their needs well, and they saw no need to convert to a European religion. Many Native American religions featured women as the creators or cocreators of the universe. For instance, in the creation story of the tribes of the Iroquois confederacy the Sky-Woman fell to earth, where she gave birth to twins. These twins filled the world with rivers, trees, mountains, and plains. Women in Native American society could become important religious figures, such as priestesses and spiritual leaders.

OPPOSITE, MAIN PICTURE: **Indians attack Anne Hutchinson and her family.**

OPPOSITE, INSET: **The trial of Anne Hutchinson. Undated woodcut.**

LEFT: **"Anne Hutchison Preaches."**

Mary Dyer

"Mary Dyer did hang as a flag for others to take example by."

General Atherton spoke these words just after Mary Dyer was hanged by the neck on Boston Common. Mary's early death was because she was a Quaker at a time when Quakers were feared as being "underminers of this government" (so said Governor Endicott when prosecuting Mary). Mary and her husband William had moved from England to Boston in 1635 and had become followers of Anne Hutchinson. Anne had been a Puritan but had become unhappy with the fact that Puritans did not believe people had a direct link to God. Anne felt that her own faith was all she needed to relate to God. This meant she was criticized by ministers like Hugh Peter in Salem for being more "a Husband than a Wife, and a preacher than a hearer."

Anne was thrown out of her church in Boston on March 22, 1638, and as she walked out alone, one woman took her hand and joined her. That woman was Mary Dyer. Mary and Anne were close friends, and Anne had helped Mary when she lost a child in 1637. Anne was a midwife, and Mary's husband called her to help when Mary went into premature labor in 1637. The child, a girl, was stillborn (dead at birth) and badly deformed. Anne and William Dyer buried the child in secret, "...as neither hog nor dog, nor any other beast may come unto it," but the secret got out and was soon held up as an example of Mary being

MARY DYER

"Anti-War Protesters Enter Boston Common" by Franklin McMahon. If you look in the background, you will see the statue of Mary Dyer standing outside the Boston State House. It is no surprise that Mary's statue now looks out on the place where people come to protest for what they believe in. Mary died because of what she believed in, and so she has become a symbol to others who feel that their cause is worth making a stand for.

44

ABOVE: **Mary Dyer, William Robinson, and Marmaduke Stevenson are led to their execution. Robinson and Stevenson were hanged, but Dyer was given a seven-month stay until her execution in 1660.**

ABOVE LEFT: **A nineteenth-century drawing of Mary Dyer being led to the gallows in Boston.**

punished by God for her religious beliefs. One pamphlet recorded the event like this:

"This year there was a hideous monster born at Boston, in New England, of one Mrs. Mary Dyer, a copartner with the said Mrs. Hutchinson…the said monster, as it was related to me, was without head, but horns like a beast, scales or a rough skin like the fish, called the horn-back; it had legs and claws like a fowl, and in other respects as a woman child; the Lord declaring

his detestation of their monstrous errors, as was then thought by some, by this prodigious [being an omen or a sign] birth."

Mary and her husband moved away from Boston and then back to England. By the time Mary returned to Boston in 1656, the Puritan government was worried about the disruption that Quakers could cause. As a result, harsh new rules had been put in place to stop Quakers from entering the city. Quakers preached a religion that did not need the strict levels of church hierarchy on which the Puritans insisted. Mary was found as her ship docked in Boston harbor and thrown in jail, but released after her husband wrote to the governors of Boston. A condition of Mary's release was that she never be allowed to enter Massachusetts again. This was a rule that Mary could not live by—twice more she entered Boston to beg for the release of her fellow Quakers, and twice more she was imprisoned and released after her husband wrote to the governors.

When Mary and her fellow Quakers were asked why they continued to return to Boston, they replied, "…the ground and cause of their coming was of the Lord." Told by Governor Endicott that she would hang for her beliefs, Mary stood firm, and she replied:

"Yea, and joyfully I go."

On June 1, 1660, Mary was led from her prison cell and paraded through the streets to the gallows on Boston Common. Drummers walked in front and behind her to make sure no one could hear her if she spoke to the crowd. Many in the crowd called out for Mary to repent and be saved, but Mary would not. Her Quaker beliefs were more important to her than her life. In death she hoped to promote her beliefs to more people by becoming a martyr to the Quaker cause. As Mary said:

"My Life not Availeth Me In Comparison to the Liberty of the Truth."

45

> **❝I am no more a witch than you are a wizard, and if you take away my life God will give you blood to drink.❞**

Sarah Good's "curse" on Minister Nicholas Noyes at her execution in Salem in 1692 was said, by some, to have come true when the minister later died of internal bleeding. Many saw this as ultimate proof that Sarah had been a witch. She was one of the first three women to be accused of witchcraft in Salem during a time that has now become famous in the town's history.

The Salem witch trials
Between June and September 1692, 20 people, mostly women, were executed as witches, and hundreds more were accused. All this started with the seemingly innocent accusations of a group of teenage girls in Salem. However, the witch hunts soon became a reason for people to punish women who didn't fit in for one reason or another. Sarah Good was a prime example: At the time of her accusation she was a homeless mother, married to a man who thought nothing of calling her "an enemy to all good" at her trial. She was not well liked by her neighbors because of her habit of swearing at them when they denied her charity. At Sarah's trial her neighbors lined up to complain about her and were

quick to link any misfortune to Sarah's witchcraft.

Samuel and Mary Abbey had evicted Sarah from the house she rented from them a few years earlier "for Quitteness sake." They wasted no time at Sarah's trial in blaming the deaths of their farm animals since that time on Sarah:

> "The winter following after the said Sarah was gone from our hose, we began to Loose Cattle, and Lost severall after an unusuall Manner…Lost after that manner 17 head of Cattle within two years, besides Sheep, and Hoggs; and both do believe they Died by witchcraft."

Soon, unpopular women in villages near Salem also found themselves accused by spiteful neighbors. Many pamphlets were written and sermons given warning of the horrors of witches. Cotton Mather, the Puritan preacher, wrote an essay in 1692 called *The Wonders of*

ABOVE: **A young woman, accused of witchcraft in Salem, tries to defend herself. Complaints by neighbors led to the conviction and execution of innocent women.**

BELOW: **Title page of Cotton Mather's book on witchcraft. Pamphlets such as this served to fuel the great witch hunts.**

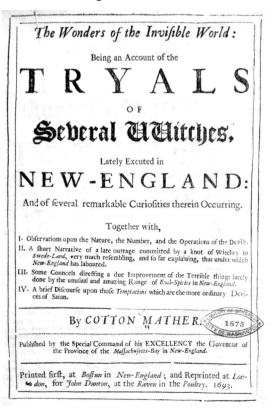

ABOVE: **Burning was a common way to kill those suspected of witchcraft. It was thought that the evil powers of a witch could only be removed if the witch was killed by fire.**

the Invisible World, in which he noted that:

"The Devil has made a dreadful Knot of Witches in the Country...these Witches...do all sorts of Mischiefs to the Neighbors...at prodigious Witch-meetings, the Wretches have proceeded so far, as to Concert and Consult the Methods of Rooting out the Christian Religion from this Country, and setting up instead of it, perhaps a more gross Diabolism [devil worship], than ever the World saw before."

Such witch hunts had previously happened all over Europe and are now seen by historians as being a sign of the religious and social unrest of the seventeenth century. In the end everyone was so terrified of being accused of witchcraft that they were quick to blame anyone else.

The following year the antiwitch hysteria started to die down, and Increase Mather (father of Cotton) voiced his concern about the killing of innocent women as witches:

"It were better that ten suspected witches should escape than that one innocent person should be condemned."

Thirteen years later, in 1706, Ann Putnam, one of the original teenage accusers, finally admitted that she had lied:

"I desire to be humbled before God. It was a great delusion of Satan that deceived me in that sad time. I did it not out of any anger, malice, or ill will...I desire to lie in the dust and earnestly beg forgiveness of all those I have given just cause of sorrow and offense, and whose relations were taken away and accused."

WOMEN AND SLAVERY

❝It is likewise most lamentable to think, how in taking Negroes out of Africa and selling of them here, that which God has joined together men do boldly rent asunder—men from their wives, parents from their children.❞

Samuel Sewall was clearly not in favor of the slave trade when he wrote *The Sin of Slaveholding* in 1700. His words describe what must have been the first, and perhaps the biggest, blow to African women arriving in America at this time. In most cases their children and husbands were taken from them to be sold separately. Very often the family never saw each other again.

For those women who gave birth to children in slavery, the colonial farmer and writer J. Hector St. John de Crevecouer paints a bleak picture of their fate:

"They have no time, like us, tenderly to rear their helpless offspring, to nurse them on their knees, to enjoy the delight of being parents…if their children live, they must live to be slaves like themselves…the mothers must fasten them on their backs, and, with this double load, follow their husbands in the fields, where they too often hear no other sound than that of the voice or whip of the task-master, and the cries of their infants, broiling in the sun. These unfortunate creatures cry and weep like their parents, without a possibility of relief."

Origins of the slave trade
The first Africans came to American soil in 1619, their ship landing in Jamestown, Virginia. At this time African Americans often worked under similar contracts as white indentured servants. They had to work for between four and seven years, then they

48

were declared free. This meant that by the midseventeenth century there were free African Americans living in the colonies. As the economy in the colonies grew, so did the need for slaves. Africans were brought over in ever increasing numbers and set to work on plantations and farms. There they were responsible for planting, harvesting, and processing cotton, tobacco, sugar, and rice, and working as household servants and craftsmen. By 1750 there were more than 200,000 Africans being used as slaves in America. By 1800 that number had more than tripled. When the European settlers started to realize how much their fortunes relied on this African workforce, they tightened the rules surrounding freedom. From 1640 onward African American workers were

no longer treated as indentured servants who would become free after a period of time. They were now slaves—property that could be bought and sold.

The worth of women

At first it was mainly men who were brought from Africa as slaves. Male slaves were worth the most money, and until the 1660s there were two African men brought to the New World for every one African woman. Before long, however, slave owners started to see how women could be even more useful than men. First, they were cheaper to buy than men. Also, women could carry out most of the labor done by men as well as countless domestic chores. In addition to working in the fields, they could cook, clean, nurse children, weave, and sew.

ABOVE: **Slaves picking cotton on a plantation in around 1800. The women and men would work together in the fields.**

OPPOSITE, ABOVE: **American poet Phillis Wheatley (1753–1784) was bought as a slave by Mr. John Wheatley of Boston. She quickly became an accomplished writer and in 1773 published a volume entitled *Poems on Various Subjects, Religious and Moral*. This was a remarkable achievement for any woman at that time, but it was even more astonishing for an African American woman who had been sold as a slave.**

LEFT: **Slaves on a cotton plantation working a cotton gin in about 1800. Men and women worked together on jobs like this, with women doing as much heavy work as the men.**

LEFT: **An overseer is watching the work of these slaves in a Texas cotton field. Women were expected to carry out heavy manual labor —pregnancy was no excuse for slacking.**

And most crucially, they could give birth. The Virginia Slave Laws of 1662 stated:

> "Whereas some doubts have arisen whether children got by any Englishman upon a Negro woman should be slave or free, be it therefore enacted and declared by this present Grand Assembly, that all children born in this country shall be held bond or free only according to the condition of the mother."

That is to say, any children born to a slave woman would be slaves whether their fathers were slaves or slave masters. So a slave owner could increase the number of his slaves simply by making the women bear children.

Very few Africans were literate when they first arrived in America, so most available primary sources are written about slaves rather than by them. The sources show us the misery that these African women must have gone through. For instance, take a look at these entries from the journal of William Byrd:

> "February 8, 1709…I ate milk for breakfast. I said my prayers. Jenny and Eugene were whipped. I danced my dance...
> "February 22, 1709…I threatened Anaka with a whipping if she did not confess the intrigues between Daniel and Nurse, but she prevented by a confession. I chided Nurse severely about it...
> "September 3, 1709…In the afternoon I beat Jenny for throwing water on the couch…
> "June 17, 1710…I ate tongue and chicken for dinner. In the afternoon…Jenny was whipped…
> "February 27, 1711…In the evening my wife and little Jenny had a great quarrel in which my wife got the worst but at last by the help of the family Jenny was overcome and soundly whipped."

The violent punishments given to his slave women were clearly just part of William's daily routine. The lives of Anaka and Jenny must have been filled with fear of their cruel owner.

Hope and freedom
By the middle of the eighteenth century the African American population had grown so much that most plantations had large slave communities. Within these groups African American women could find husbands. The pleasures of family life could go some way toward making their lives more bearable. Meg and Venture Smith met while working for a Mr. Mumford in New York. Venture records that in 1751:

> "I married Meg, a slave of his who was about my age."

In marrying other slaves, slave women sometimes gained more than a husband—they also gained the possibility of freedom. There are recorded cases of slave men buying their own freedom and then saving enough money to buy back their wives. In Venture Smith's remarkable narrative he tells of how he bought his own freedom in 1765 at the age of 36. He then went on to earn enough money to buy back his family, first his two sons and:

"In my forty-fourth year, I purchased my wife Meg, and thereby prevented having another child to buy, as she was then pregnant. I gave forty pounds for her."

Lucy Terry Prince, the first African American poet, was sold into slavery as an infant. In 1756 she married a free African man called Abijah Prince, who purchased Lucy's freedom. Lucy and Abijah went on to have six children. They moved to Guilford, Vermont, and purchased land. In the 1790s the Prince family became involved in a land dispute with Colonel Eli Bronson. Lucy took the case all the way to the Supreme Court, where she argued it herself and won. This was an outstanding feat for a woman at this time—especially an African American woman who had started her time as a slave.

BELOW: **Illustrations showing African American life in the South in 1807. Top: "Southern cotton plantation" showing African American workers picking cotton. Bottom: "Southern Negro quarter" showing an African American village and people.**

WOMEN ABOLITIONISTS

Not all white colonial Americans were in favor of slavery, and toward the end of the eighteenth century the voices of those opposed to the barbaric trade became louder. In 1800 a group of American women wrote an *Appeal to Women on the Subject of the Abolition of Slavery*. In it they expressed their feelings, as women, for the women experiencing the horrors of slavery and vowed to do all they can to see it abolished:

"With the system of slavery as it now exists in our country, a band of fearless and true hearted patriots have declared open and eternal war, and as American females, daughters of the Pilgrim Fathers, and mothers of the future defenders of our beloved land, we have come up with them to the contest, never to lay aside our armor until the sacred cause of liberty is triumphant, or we are sacrificed in the struggle…in behalf of woman, publicly exposed for sale under circumstances the most revolting to human nature, or woman bleeding under the torturing lash, trampled into the very dust of humiliation, scorned, polluted, ruined both for time and eternity! We are daughters, and we must feel for the daughter… As wives we feel for the wife… As mothers…we feel for that miserable mother, doomed as she often is, to drag out a joyless existence deprived of all that could render life tolerable."

Elizabeth Freeman

❝Elizabeth Freeman known by the name of MUMBET Died Dec. 28, 1829. Her supposed age was 85 Years. She was born a slave and remained a slave for nearly thirty years. She could neither read nor write, yet in her own sphere she had no superior nor equal. She neither wasted time nor property. She never violated a trust, nor failed to perform a duty. In every situation of domestic trial, she was the most efficient helper, and the tenderest friend. Good Mother, farewell.❞

Charles Sedgwick wrote this epitaph on the gravestone of his mother, Elizabeth Freeman, a woman whose story is one of remarkable courage. Elizabeth was born into slavery, of African parents, and as a child she was given to Colonel John Ashley by his parents-in-law. Elizabeth, known later as Mum Bett or Mumbet, went to work for Colonel Ashley at his house in Sheffield, Massachusetts, with her sister Lizzie. There is evidence that Lizzie had learning difficulties, and Elizabeth was very protective of her. This account by one of the children of Theodore Sedgwick (later Elizabeth's lawyer) shows how Elizabeth's protectiveness started a chain of events that some say was the foundation of the civil rights movement:

"While Mum Bett resided in the family of Col. Ashley, she received a severe wound in a generous attempt to shield her sister. Her mistress in a fit of passion resorted to a degree and mode of violence very uncommon in this country: she struck at the weak and timid [Lizzie] with a heated kitchen shovel: mum Bett interposed her arm, and received the blow; and bore the honorable scar it left to the day of her death."

This incident made Elizabeth think long and hard about her state of slavery—something that many slave women no doubt did, but few of them made the decision that Elizabeth did. Elizabeth had recently heard the words of the Declaration of Independence, and they made her think about her own rights. She is reported to have visited Theodore Sedgwick, a local lawyer, and said:

"I heard that paper read yesterday that says all men are born equal, and that every man has a right to freedom...I am not a dumb critter; won't the law give me any freedom?"

Elizabeth had more reason than most to expect some rights of her own from this new state of independence because her own husband had been killed in the

Revolutionary War. Theodore Sedgwick agreed with Elizabeth that she had a case, and he resolved to help her and another slave man named Brom sue for freedom.

The case of *Brom & Bett v. Ashley* appeared in the courts in August 1781. The fact that Sedgwick would act as the defender of a slave woman was a brave move, but Elizabeth's bravery in standing up for rights that she had not yet been granted was unheard of at that time. Sedgwick and his colleague Tapping Reeve argued that the Declaration of Independence rendered slavery illegal, and the courts agreed with him. Elizabeth was granted her freedom and went to work in the Sedgwick household, where she worked as a nurse and housekeeper. It was here that she took on the surname "Freeman." Freedom was important enough to Elizabeth to risk everything for, as she made clear in a later statement:

"Any time, any time while I was a slave, if one minute's freedom had been offered to me, and I had been told I must die at the end of that minute, I would have taken it—just to stand one minute on god' airth [earth] a free woman—I would."

Elizabeth was the first slave to win her own freedom through the law courts, and her case started the ball rolling for the abolition of slavery in Massachusetts.

LEFT: **This portrait of Elizabeth Freeman was painted on ivory by Susan Ridley Sedgwick when Elizabeth was nearly 70 years old. Susan was the daughter-in-law of the lawyer who had represented Elizabeth in her fight for freedom.**
© Massachusetts Historical Society, Boston, MA, USA/Bridgeman Art Library

OPPOSITE LEFT: **The tombstone of Elizabeth Freeman, which still stands in the old burial ground of Stockbridge.**

> **❝Let the Daughters of Liberty nobly arise;
> And though we've no voice but a negative here,
> The use of the taxables, let us forbear...
> Stand firmly resolv'd, and bid Grenville to see,
> That rather than freedom we part with our tea,
> And well as we love the dear draught when a-dry,
> As American Patriots our taste we deny.❞**

This popular poem from 1768 was dedicated to the Daughters of Liberty during the Revolutionary War. It sums up the feelings of many women at this turbulent time, who were desperate to find some way of helping America's cause in her fight for independence from Britain. Women had two main choices at this time: Either to stay at home while their husbands, fathers, brothers, and sons went off to fight (for one side or the other), or to go with their men-folk to battle.

Running the wartime household

For those who chose to stay at home, life became harder than ever. To keep the money coming in, women had to take over the wage-earning roles of their husbands. This meant learning new skills and entering a business world that had previously been all male. Women became printers, blacksmiths, store-keepers, and farmers. In the evenings they continued to carry out all the chores that kept their households running, as well as raising families as single parents. Abigail Adams, wife of John Adams, a leading revolutionary and later the second president of the United States, wrote to her husband and told him how worried she was about coping in his absence:

> "I miss my partner, and find myself uneaquil [unequal; or inadequate] to the cares which fall upon me; I find it necessary to be the directress of our Husbandery and farming."

In addition to running the household and farm, Abigail had to act as hostess and part-time nurse to the many soldiers and civilians who sought refuge:

> "Our House has been…in the same scene of confusion that it was upon the first—Soldiers coming in for lodging, for Breakfast, for Supper, for Drink &c. &c. Sometimes refugees from Boston tired and fatigued, seek an assilum [asylum] for a Day or Night, a week—you can hardly imagine how we live."

Abigail had the same strength of spirit as her husband and reassured him:

> "We are no ways dispirited here, we possess a Spirit that will not be conquered. If our Men are all drawn of and we should be attacked, you would find a Race of Amazons in America."

For some women the extra responsibility made them feel differently about their traditional role. In a letter from Lucy Knox to her husband Henry Knox, one of Washington's generals, she advises him:

> "I hope you will not consider yourself as commander in chief of your own house, but be convinced that there is such a thing as equal command."

A political voice

Wealthy society women found the revolutionary cause a reason to have a voice in politics for the first time. During the war Esther Reed created the Ladies' Association of Philadelphia and wrote a pamphlet called *Sentiments of an American Woman*:

> "If opinion and manners did not forbid us to march to glory by the same paths as the Men, we should at least equal, and sometimes surpass them in our love for the public good....Who, amongst us, will not renounce with the highest pleasure, those vain ornaments, when-she shall consider that the valiant defenders of America will be able to draw some advantage from the money which she may have laid out in these...that these presents will perhaps be valued by them at a greater price, when they will have it in their power to say: This is the offering of the Ladies."

By refusing to buy British goods and

ABOVE: **Mary Ludwig Hays McCauley (1754–1832), stoking a cannon for the Pennsylvania artillery in the Battle of Monmouth in New Jersey during the Revolutionary War, June 1778. She replaced her fallen husband, John Hays, as a cannon loader.**

BELOW LEFT: **October 7, 1777: Christina Henrietta Caroline Ackland (1750–1815) travels down the Hudson to General Gates's camp for a pass to cross the lines to nurse her husband, British Major Ackland, wounded in the second Battle of Saratoga.**

collecting money to send to the revolutionary cause, women got closer than ever to playing a part in politics.

Following and fighting

Some women chose to follow their men to war. These women had a choice—either follow the camp or go in disguise and fight alongside the men. Those women who became camp followers carried out many

LEFT: **Helping hands. Elizabeth Zane running back with powder from her brother's house to help the besieged Fort Henry at Wheeling, Virginia, in 1777.**

BELOW LEFT: **Mrs. Robert Murray, a Quaker mother, served cakes and wine to Henry Clinton's British officers after their landing at Kip's Bay in New York in order to delay their interception of American forces, September 15, 1776.**

jobs in support of the army and were an officially recognized part of the army. They often took children with them, who also did tasks like carrying gunpowder and water. Women cooked and cleaned for the soldiers, nursed the injured, carried messages, and often found themselves in grave danger from enemy troops. The women had to keep up with the soldiers on the march, even though they also had to carry pots, pans, baggage, and children. Some women even gave birth along the way.

There were concerns at times that the number of women camp followers had become too large. So, Captain John Knox of the 43rd Regiment made this note about the rations that women should receive:

"Provisions are issued to the women upon a presumption that they are to be useful to the soldiers, either by attending hospitals or by washing for them and the officers."

There is much evidence that the women were useful, however. Just read this

ABOVE: **Catherine van Rensselaer Schuyler, wife of General Philip Schuyler, set fire to her cornfields to delay the approach of the British. Women left alone to tend farms often had to make major decisions like this in order to protect themselves, their family, and their farm.**

account of the American army around Boston in 1775:

> "They have no women in the camp to do washing for the men, and they in general not being used to doing things of this sort…choose rather to let their linen, etc., rot upon their backs than be at the trouble of cleaning 'em themselves."

Women were not allowed to fight as soldiers during the Revolutionary War, so those who wanted to get involved sometimes went so far as to disguise themselves as men. As strange as this seems, there are many records of women doing this. One famous example was Deborah Sampson, whose story can be read in the next section on pages 58-59. Other women made spontaneous attempts to attack British soldiers or to help the American army in their efforts against the enemy.

Margaret Cochran Corbin started out as a camp follower helping her husband John's regiment. On November 16, 1776, John and Margaret were stationed in Fort Washington, New York, when they were attacked by British troops. John was killed as he tried to fire a cannon. Margaret quickly moved into John's place and continued to load and fire the cannon until she, too, was injured by grapeshot (small iron balls fired from a cannon) and lost the use of her left arm. In 1779 Margaret became the first woman to be awarded a military pension as a reward for her bravery.

A slow revolution for women

When America finally earned its victory over the British in 1783, the world had changed for American women. Although liberty and equality were not immediately granted to women, most had experienced what it was like to have more of a voice than before. Although most returned to their domestic roles after the war, all the advances made could not be turned back. More girls started to go to school than ever before, and more women ran businesses, some out of choice rather than necessity. It would be wrong to say that there was a sense of "women's rights," but the seeds had been sown for change. Abigail Adams wrote to her husband in 1776, setting out what she hoped for from a state of independence:

> "I desire you would Remember the Ladies, and be more generous…to them than your ancestors. Do not put such unlimited power into the hands of the Husbands. Remember all Men would be tyrants if they could. If perticuliar [particular] care and attention is not paid to the Ladies we are determined to foment a Rebellion, and will not hold ourselves bound by any Laws in which we have no voice, or Representation."

Deborah Sampson

> **"My mind became agitated with the enquiry— why a nation, separated from us by an ocean [should] enforce on us plans of subjugation."**

Deborah Sampson wrote these words to explain her extraordinary behavior during the Revolutionary War. Deborah felt so strongly that her country should be free from British rule that she decided to join the army and:

> "Become one of the severest avengers of the wrong."

However, there was a problem. At this time women were not allowed to become soldiers, so Deborah had to dress as a young man in order to join the army. Early in 1782 Deborah decided to test whether she would be able to pass herself off as a man by dressing in man's clothing and going to her local tavern. No one seemed to notice she was not a man, so Deborah signed up for the army under the name Timothy Thayer from Carver. It is said that while Deborah was signing the Articles of Enlistment in the town, a Mrs. Wood remarked:

> "Thayer holds the quill with his finger in that funny position, like Deborah Sampson."

Oddly, no one noticed that it was Deborah enlisting in the army. There is evidence, however, that some people were suspicious. Deborah had recently renounced her Puritan faith and had become a Baptist. We know that she was later banned from the First Baptist Church of Middleboro, Massachusetts, because of rumors that she was "Dressing in man's clothes and enlisting as a Soldier in the Army."

On May 20 of that year Deborah enlisted in the Fourth Massachusetts Regiment of the Continental Army, masquerading as a young man named Robert Shurtleff (the name of her brother, who had died at the age of eight). This was a risky decision, because not only would people be horrified if they found out, but it also meant that Deborah was putting herself in grave danger. Luckily, Deborah was a strong young woman. She had been an indentured servant for eight years, doing hard labor in the fields. She had learned to shoot with her master's sons in the woods around the farm and was well equipped to survive the harsh life of a soldier. Deborah's biggest fear was not the enemy but that she would be discovered and sent home in shame. Deborah bound her breasts, tied back her hair, and at 5 foot 7 inches could easily pass as a "smock-faced" man too young to shave.

Deborah's regiment was stationed at West Point in New York, and it was there

BELOW: **Deborah Sampson (center) disguised herself as a man in order to fight.**

had proved herself to be as valuable a soldier as any man, society was not yet ready to accept a woman soldier, no matter how passionate she was about the cause for which she fought.

BELOW: **Deborah Sampson as she usually looked when not dressed as a man.**

that Deborah was first injured, shot in the leg. She was so worried that the doctors would discover her secret that she decided to nurse the leg herself—it never fully recovered. She was injured twice more—a sword cut to the head and a bullet in her thigh—but she never allowed herself to be properly treated. Eventually she became very ill with a fever and was sent to a hospital in Philadelphia. While Deborah was ill, the doctor found out that she was a woman, but he did not say anything to Deborah's officers until she had fully recovered.

Finally, Deborah was summoned to General Washington's office, where her secret was revealed, and she was discharged from the army. Although Deborah

DEBORAH SAMPSON.

Published by H. Mann, 1797.

WOMEN AND POLITICS

> ❝We cannot be indifferent on any occasion that appears nearly to affect the peace and happiness of our country.❞

These words, written by the women of Edenton, North Carolina, in 1774, show how keen many women were to play a part in political life. However, in early America women and politics did not—and could not—mix. Women were simply thought to be incapable of the mind-power and rationality needed of people in politics. This, obviously, was not true; but at a time when women did not have the power to vote or to become involved in the world of higher education, they did not have much opportunity to prove men wrong. Politics was also thought of as unfem-inine. Women were sup-posed to occupy their thoughts with domestic matters—children and the home. Then some-thing happened that opened an opportunity for women to become involved in the polit-ical world—the Rev-olutionary War.

At this time women were serious consum-ers of British products

—they used British cloth for their dresses, they drank British tea, and those who could afford it served British delicacies at their table. When the British Stamp Act of 1765 imposed a tax on all legal documents used in America, the colonies reacted angrily. The resulting protests to this "taxation without representation" included agree-ments by several colonies to stop importing British goods, and women were soon involved in the protests.

The Edenton tea party

On October 25, 1774, Penelope Barker of Edenton, North Carolina, invited 50 of her friends to come to her house for a tea party with a difference. This was a political gathering—the women wrote a document that stated they would support the quest for independence from Britain and would not buy tea or cloth from Britain until the tax laws were removed:

> "It is a duty which we owe, not only to our near and dear connections…but to ourselves who are essentially interested in their welfare, to do every thing as far as lies in our power to testify our sincere adherence to the same; and we do therefore accordingly subscribe this paper, as a witness of our fixed intention and solemn determination to do so."

This was a brave act for women at this time, and even more bravely, they all signed the document. The actions of the women of Edenton were even reported in Britain, where the *Morning Chronicle and London Advertiser* of January 16, 1775, wrote an admiring account of the event:

> "The Provincial Deputies of North Carolina having resolved not to drink any more tea, nor wear any more British cloth, &c. Many ladies of this Province have determined to give a memorable proof of their patriotism, and have accordingly entered into the following honorable and spirited association. I send it to you, to show your fair countrywomen, how zealously and faithfully American ladies follow the laudable example of their husbands,

Two political wives: LEFT **Martha Washington (1731–1802), wife of George Washington and** BELOW LEFT **a silhouette of Martha Jefferson (1748-82).**

TOP: **A romanticized image of Betsy making the flag.**

ABOVE: **Betsy Ross's flag.**

ABOVE LEFT: **The Betsy Ross House, Philadelphia, Pennsylvania.**

and what opposition your Ministers may expect to receive from a people thus firmly united against them."

Fit for politics

Many women knew a great deal about politics at this time because they were often unnoticed guests at political meetings. Many meetings took place in boarding houses, coffeehouses, and salons that belonged to, or were run by, women. Women must have been frustrated that they were expected to remain silent at these meetings. This was something expressed by Judith Sargent Stevens Murray in her book *On the Equality of the Sexes* in 1790. Judith felt that a new republic should also involve a new, equal role for women. She believed that if women were allowed the same education as men, they would prove themselves just as fit for politics:

"Is the needle and kitchen sufficient to employ the operations of a soul...? I should conceive not....Are we deficient in reason? We can only reason from what we know, and if an opportunity of acquiring knowledge hath been denied us, the inferiority of our sex cannot fairly be deduced from thence."

Unfortunately for women then, Judith's views were clearly far ahead of their time. Equality for women and their accepted role in politics was nearly two centuries away.

BETSY ROSS

While it was not a political act, a woman created one of the best-known symbols of American independence in June 1776. Elizabeth Griscom Ross—better known as Betsy Ross—was a seamstress who knew George and Martha Washington. Betsy Ross's niece later told the story of how Betsy made the first American flag:

"She made it on the order of General Washington, who called personally upon her at her house...they brought with them a drawing...of the proposed flag; that she said it was wrong, and proposed alterations one of these alterations was in regard to the number of points of the star; that she said it should be five-pointed...and the committee carried it before Congress, by whom it was approved and adopted."

> **❝I am obnoxious to each carping tongue
> Who says my hand a needle better fits,
> A poet's pen all scorn I should thus wrong,
> For such despite they cast on female wits:
> If what I do prove well, it won't advance,
> They'll say it's stolen, or else it was by
> chance....Men can do best, and women know
> it well. Preeminence in all and each is
> yours—Yet grant some small
> acknowledgment of ours.❞**

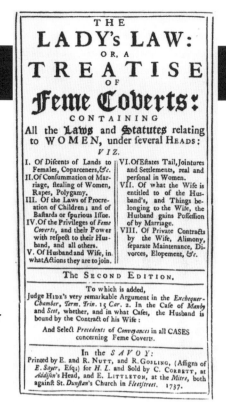

THE
LADY's LAW:
OR, A
TREATISE
OF
Feme Coverts:
CONTAINING
All the Laws and Statutes relating
to WOMEN, under several HEADS:
VIZ.

I. Of Difcents of Lands to Females, Coparceners, &c.
II. Of Confummation of Marriage, ftealing of Women, Rapes, Polygamy.
III. Of the Laws of Procreation of Children; and of Baftards or fpurious Iffue.
IV. Of the Privileges of *Feme Coverts,* and their Power with refpect to their Hufband, and all others.
V. Of Husband and Wife, in what Actions they are to join.
VI. Of Eftates Tail, Jointures and Settlements, real and perfonal in Women.
VII. Of what the Wife is entitled to of the Hufband's, and Things belonging to the Wife, the Husband gains Poffeffion of by Marriage.
VIII. Of Private Contracts by the Wife, Alimony, feparate Maintenance, Divorces, Elopement, &c.

The SECOND EDITION.

To which is added,
Judge HIDE's very remarkable Argument in the *Exchequer-Chamber, Term. Trin.* 15 *Car.* 2. In the Cafe of *Manby* and *Scot,* whether, and in what Cafes, the Husband is bound by the Contract of his Wife:

And Select *Precedents* of *Conveyances* in all CASES concerning Feme Coverts.

In the *SAVOY:*
Printed by E. and R. NUTT, and R. GOSLING, (Affigns of *E. Sayer,* Efq;) for H. L. and Sold by C. CORBETT, at *Addifon's* Head, and E. LITTLETON, at the *Mitre,* both against St. *Dunftan's* Church in *Fleetftreet.* 1737.

The feeling behind these lines, written by the colonial poet Anne Bradstreet in 1650, is clear. Anne is arguing that women's achievements should not be overlooked by men simply because women were considered inferior. This verse was written at a time when women were seen as inferior to men not only by society but by the legal system, too. When the first settlers arrived in the New World from England in the seventeenth century, they brought many things with them from their homeland, including the legal system. Under this system women lost all legal rights as soon as they married—a system called coverture. This meant that women had to rely on their husbands for any legal

ABOVE: **There were different laws for women and men at this time, and this pamphlet printed in 1737 spelled out all the laws that applied to women.**

LEFT: **Mary Wollstonecraft wrote a book called *A Vindication of the Rights of Women* in 1792. It was one of the first books to argue for equal rights for women.**

agreement, and everything the woman had owned before marriage—from jewelry and clothing to property—now belonged to her husband. This was considered to be a normal state of affairs because men were considered far more capable and important than women when it came to legal matters. In his book *The Married Lady's Companion,* published in 1808, Samuel Jennings sums up attitudes toward women in marriage:

"Marriage rests on a condition of a loving and cheerful submission on

ABOVE: **Engraving of a New York "dive," with men and women dancing and drinking, 1800s.**

the part of the wife. Here again you object and say, 'Why not the husband, first show a little condescension as well as the wife?' I answer for these plain reasons. It is not his disposition; it is not the custom but with the henpecked; it is not his duty; it is not implied in the marriage contract; it is not required by law or gospel…when you became a wife, he became your head, and your supposed superiority was buried in that voluntary act."

Education for women

Most women put up with the legal system of coverture because it was the normal state of affairs. However, there is evidence that some women were frustrated by this lack of recognition in the eyes of the law. In 1792 an Englishwoman named Mary Wollstonecraft wrote *A Vindication of the Rights of Woman*. Mary was one of the first women to openly call for equal education of men and women. She believed that the only reason women were inferior to men was because they were not given the same educational opportunities as men, and that the legal power of men meant women were kept downtrodden:

"Many are the causes that, in the present corrupt state of society, contribute to enslave women by cramping their understandings and sharpening their senses….But avoiding, as I have hitherto done, any direct comparison of the two sexes collectively, or frankly acknowledging the inferiority of woman, according to the present appearance of things, I shall only insist that men have increased that inferiority till women are almost sunk below the standard of rational creatures.…The laws respecting woman, which I mean to discuss in a future part, make an absurd unit of a man and his wife; and then, by the easy transition of only considering him as responsible, she is reduced to a mere cipher [nonentity]."

Many men, and women too, criticized Mary for such radical thoughts, but she was not the only one championing more rights for women. Daniel Defoe, the English writer (best known as the author of *Robinson Crusoe*) whose works were also read in the New World, wrote *On the Education of Women* in 1719. He, like Mary, felt that women would be capable of just as much as men if only they were given as much education:

"I have often thought of it as one of the most barbarous customs in the

world, considering us as a civilized and a Christian country, that we deny the advantages of learning to women. We reproach the sex every day with folly and impertinence [rudeness]; while I am confident, had they the advantages of education equal to us, they would be guilty of less than ourselves."

You read in the previous section about Judith Sargent Stevens Murray's book *On the Equality of the Sexes*. Born in 1751, Judith was largely self-educated. She started writing in 1774, and some of her works were published in popular Massachusetts journals, although Judith wrote under assumed names so that her ideas would not be rejected out of hand:

"Yes, ye lordly, ye haughty sex, our souls are by nature equal to yours; the same breath of God animates, enlivens, and invigorates us…we

are not fallen lower than yourselves.…I dare confidently believe, that from the commencement of time to the present day, there hath been as many females, as males, who, by the mere force of natural powers, have merited the crown of applause; who thus unassisted, have seized the wreath of fame.…"

It must be remembered that women like Judith were very unusual at this time.

The feme sole

Most women would never have dared speak out for more legal rights. The only alternative that women had to coverture was to be a "feme sole." A feme sole (from the French for "single woman") was a woman over 21 who had not yet married and therefore had retained her legal rights. Or, more unusually, it was a married woman whose husband had agreed to let her keep her legal rights.

ABOVE: **Illustration of a room in Fraunces Tavern, an inn owned by Samuel Francis (1722–95) in New York City.**

RIGHT: **One place where women did vote after the Revolutionary War was in New Jersey, where the first constitution of 1776 gave the vote to "all inhabitants of this colony, of full age, who are worth fifty pounds…and have resided within the county…for twelve months." This meant in practice that unmarried women (because married women were represented by their husbands) voted. In 1807 the state's legislature ignored the constitution and restricted suffrage to white male citizens who paid taxes.**

An example of a typical feme sole in colonial America was Margaret Brent. Margaret was born in Gloucestershire, England, in 1601 and arrived in

Maryland in 1638 with her sister Mary and brothers Giles and Fulke. Margaret never married. In a society in which men outnumbered women six to one, this was very unusual. Margaret and her sister bought property and lived together. They made their money by importing and selling indentured servants, and by lending money to recently arrived settlers. Margaret made full use of her legal rights as a feme sole and even represented herself in court when collecting unpaid debts. In fact, she is recorded as being involved in no fewer than 134 legal cases between 1642 and 1650, always representing herself in court and usually winning her cases!

Margaret never relied on her brothers to help her, and before long she was well respected in the community for being a woman of property. Remember that Margaret would never have been able to purchase property, run a business, or represent herself in court if she had been married. The governor of Maryland, Leonard Calvert, became a good friend. Margaret made such a name for herself in the colony of Maryland that when, in 1648, Leonard died, he named Margaret as the legal executor of his will. This had never been done before and shows just how skilled Margaret was in legal and business matters.

At this time a civil war was going on in England, and English followers of Parliament landed in Maryland, planning to take over the colony for their cause. Many in the colony fled, were kidnapped, or were killed; barely 100 of the settlers remained. Leonard's instructions to Margaret were "take all, pay all," which meant she should take all the available money from Leonard's estate and that of his brother, Lord Baltimore (who was in England at that time), to pay the soldiers who were defending the colony. This was crucial to helping the colony survive.

Margaret showed great skill in making sure that the soldiers were paid, as well as in buying corn to make sure the colony did not starve. Lord Baltimore was not happy about Margaret selling his assets and criticized her publicly. The response he got shows us how unusually well respected Margaret was at that time:

"As for Mistress Brent's…meddling with your Lordships Estate here, we do Verily Believe…that it was better for the Colonies safety at that time in her hands then in any mans…for the Soldiers would never have treated any other with the Civility and respect …she rather deserved favor and thanks from your Honor [than] those bitter invectives [insults] you have been pleased to Express against her."

❝Remember friends the Solumn Hour I was a Mother and a Tomb: In Dreadful pains a Corps I bore; And Soon a Corps my Self became...❞

This inscription from a tombstone in Somers, Connecticut, tells of the death of Salla Barns in childbirth in 1780. As tragic as this death was, it was not uncommon at this time. Lack of medical facilities and knowledge meant that childbirth was one of the riskiest things a woman could go through. In the seventeenth and eighteenth centuries, between one and two out of every 100 childbirths resulted in the death of the mother. Remember that most women had between five and eight children. This meant that their chances of dying with one of them were as high as one in eight. Many things could go wrong in pregnancy—excessive bleeding, dehydration, convulsions—and with no hospital facilities available, there was little a midwife could do when things went really wrong. Some women even died from heavy-handed use of medical instruments in birth. At a time when nothing was ever sterilized, the risks of infection were huge.

Short lives

At this time women, on average, only lived for about 45 years. But in New England, if a woman survived childbirth,

she could often live into her sixties. A quarter of women even lived to 80. New England women had longer life expectancies than women in the southern colonies, mainly because of the climate. Forty-five years seems a short life, and a woman's life expectancy was shorter than a man's. But remember that this was an average kept low by the numerous deaths during childbirth. On the other hand, women tended to marry much younger than men, so they often outlived their husbands. In the southern colonies most marriages would be destroyed by the death of one partner within seven years.

Women were naturally very fearful of death, and any sign of illness caused them to worry that their life was near its end. At a time like this religion was a vital support, and prayer was seen as the best prevention for death. Anne Bradstreet's poem *Deliverance from Another Sore Fit*, written in the seventeenth century, demonstrates the strength of faith that women had at a time when illness could so easily carry them away:

"In my distress I sought the Lord,
When naught on earth could
comfort give,
And when my soul these things
abhorred,
Then, Lord, Thou said'st unto me,
'Live.'
Thou knowest the sorrows that I
felt;
My plaints and groans were heard
of Thee,
And how in sweat I seemed to melt
Thou help'st and Thou regardest
me."

Tuberculosis

In addition to childbirth there were many other risks to women at this time. Tuberculosis (TB), or consumption as it was known then, was a highly contagious disease that once caught was rarely cured. TB was the cause of up to a fifth of deaths in New England in the period up to the midnineteenth century, and 60 percent of TB victims were young women. Most victims died after a long period of suffering. One such victim was Mrs. Eleanor Emerson, who died aged 31 in 1808. A memoir of her life shows how medicine could hold off the symptoms of TB for a while, but the patient was rarely cured:

"He was of opinion, that she was far gone in a consumption; that she might hope for a little revival; but could not continue long. So it proved. His medicine operated so favorably, that the next morning she appeared considerably better....That day she rode more than 20 miles....But her eagerness to reach that place had carried her much beyond her strength. Indeed her spirits were so much raised, that she and her husband were greatly deceived with regard to her real strength....It is earnestly recommended to consumptive persons, that they be exceedingly cautious not to go beyond their strength, when journeying for health."

Other diseases that killed many women at this time were malaria, yellow fever, and cancer. Accidents were the cause of many deaths, too, with drowning being one of the most common. However, some women did live to what we would regard as old age—which would have been considered unusually old for colonial women. This 1787 entry from the diary of midwife Martha Ballard records the death of her mother:

"We receivd a Letter from our Friend...informing us of the Death of my honored Mother, who Departed this Life after a Short illness ye 4th inst; her Decease was the Palsy. She was Aged 72 Years."

Martha herself lived to the ripe old age of 77!

LEFT: **By 1625 starvation had killed three-quarters of the women who came to Jamestown between 1619 and 1622. This was known as the "Starving Time," and this picture shows the starving settlers.**

BELOW: **In 1809 the first operation to remove an ovarian tumor was performed by Dr. Ephraim McDowell. He removed a 22-pound tumor from 48-year-old Jane Todd Crawford without anesthetic. Jane went on to live to be 78. This painting shows the operation.**

> **After but a few short hours illness death has snatched from our sight one to whom youth and health had promised length of days....**

"But last evening I was at the house and in the society of Miss Harriott Mackey, and today I have beheld her a corpse! Mersiful God! Is it possible, that a few hours shall have effected so great a change, as that the object which but yesterday seemed so lovely and so fair to view, should today appear disgusting and become the object of our aversion."

Harriet Mackie died in South Carolina in 1804, and the diary entries of her friend, John Blake White, show how shocked he was at his 17-year-old friend's passing:

"What appears to mark this sad circumstance...with a mournful and deplorable aspect is her having been engaged to be married within the space of two weeks to Mr. Wm. Rose...who, by this sad stroke is rendered indeed wretched."

Grief and mourning

The fact that early death was more common at this time did not make it any less sad, and grieving family and friends found many ways to commemorate their dead loved one. Mourning pictures were favorite ways of remembering the dead, as were embroideries and paintings of graveyard scenes showing mourning family members. The account of the funeral of Mrs. Eleanor Emerson in 1808 shows little has changed in the format of funeral services between colonial times and today:

LEFT: **Eighteenth-century gravestones in a cemetery in Pittsburgh, Pennsylvania.**

BELOW LEFT AND BELOW: **Two illustrations of eighteenth-century funerals showing how mourners would sit in the room with the coffin, paying their last respects. The coffin lid would be open so people could look at the dead person one more time before they were buried.**

"The funeral was attended at the meeting house on the ensuing Thursday, Nov. 10. A solemn and affecting sermon was preached…to a very attentive audience, by the Rev. Mr. Moore….Her body was deposited in a tomb for a few hours; and then, agreeably to what she had requested, it was…laid by the side of her predecessor's, whose friendship she had so highly prized."

The high mortality rate at this time made funerals a sadly common sight. In fact, the tolling of church bells for funerals happened so often that it was banned in some places as a public nuisance. Some strange customs were used for inviting people to funerals at this time—in New England "warners" would go from door to door delivering invitations, along with wine, gloves, and cakes as gifts to the mourners! Funerals were also a reminder to others that their turn may not be far away, as this early nineteenth-century account of a village funeral shows:

"Funerals in the country are solemnly impressive. The stroke of death makes a wide space in the village circle, and is an awful event in the tranquil uniformity of rural life. The passing-bell tolls its knell in every ear; it steals with its pervading melancholy over every hill and vale, and saddens all the landscape."

GRAVESTONE

In the early Puritan colonies gravestones were plain and undecorated. However, as attitudes toward death changed and religion softened, gravestones became elaborately decorated. The early Puritans feared death because many were worried that their lives had not been godly enough to get eternal reward in heaven. However, by the early eighteenth century death was seen as a chance to become reunited with lost loved ones. The strong belief in the afterlife also softened the blow, because it meant that loved ones would see the deceased again in heaven. The inscription from a gravestone in Cape Cod shows the strength of belief in life after death:

"Here lyes interred ye body of Mrs Anna Russel consort to Mr Jospeh Russel who departed this life Febry ye 5 1729/30 in ye 23d year of her age and in her arm their son Leonard died ye same day aetatis 17 dayes.
Beneath this Marble Stone doth Lye
Two Subjects of Death's Tyranny
The Mother who in this Close Tomb
Sleeps with the Issue of her womb
Here Death deals Cruely you see
Who with the Fruit cuts down the Tree
Yet is his Malice all in vain
For Tree and Fruit shall Spring again."

ABOVE: **Harriet Newell was an American missionary who traveled to Calcutta, India, in 1812. She died in childbirth.**

Abolitionist The name given to someone who wanted to do away with slavery.

Baptist A member of the Protestant religion who believes that people have to confess their faith before they can be baptized, and that baptism should involve immersing the whole body in holy water.

Boardinghouse A place where people could rent rooms to live in.

Courtship An old-fashioned word for dating. Courtship was the period of time that a man "courted" a woman before asking her to marry him.

Coverture The legal state of a married woman. Coverture meant that the wife had to hand over all legal rights to her husband on marrying him.

Equality Total fairness between men and women under which women and men are treated the same.

Family tree A family's ancestors, as plotted out on paper or on a computer.

Feme sole The legal state of an unmarried woman. From the French *femme sole*, meaning single woman. A feme sole was allowed to buy and sell property, sign contracts, and even speak in court.

Garden of Eden In the Bible the Garden of Eden was the place where Adam and Eve first lived. It was there that Adam and Eve ate from the tree of knowledge. This is known as the "original sin."

Indentured servant A person who was bound by contract to work for between four and seven years in return for transportation to America, plus food and lodging while they worked.

Infant mortality The death of a very young child. Children are normally described as infants until they are about two or three years old.

Literary society A group of people who meet to talk about literature and to debate certain questions, usually moral or religious subjects. In the eighteenth and nineteenth centuries literary societies were usually made up of wealthy young women.

Martyr Someone who dies for something they believe in, often for religious beliefs. Martyrs are usually celebrated after their death by others who believe in the same things as they did.

Midwife Someone who assists women in childbirth. These days midwives are medical professionals, and they can be male or female. In history midwives were usually women who had no formal training but lots of experience in childbirth.

Missionary Someone whose religious faith causes them to go and work abroad. Missionaries try to convert the people they help to follow the same religion.

Persecution (religious) The physical or mental punishment of someone because of their religious beliefs.

Plantation An estate where crops are cultivated and harvested, often by slaves in early America. Typical crops grown on plantations include sugar, cotton, tobacco, and flax.

Prenuptial agreement A contract signed between a man and a woman before marriage that makes rules about what will happen to the ownership of property in the marriage.

Primary source A historical document written by someone who was present at the event or period being studied. Primary sources give firsthand evidence.

Puritan A member of the Protestant religion in the sixteenth and seventeenth centuries who wanted to make the moral rules of the religion stricter. Puritans did not like fancy church services and wanted to simplify the external elements of their religious faith.

ABOVE: **Quakers on their way to church.**

Quaker A Christian religion started in England by George Fox in 1650. Quakers have no system of church government, since all Quakers are considered to be equal in the church. Quakers believe in a direct spiritual link between God and his worshippers.

Seamstress A woman who sews clothing for money.

Smallpox A very contagious, often fatal, disease. Smallpox victims often vomit, and have pustules that leave scars.

Spinning (yarn) Materials like cotton and wool are turned into yarn by spinning. The strands of raw material are twisted using either a machine or someone spinning a small wooden top.

Tuberculosis An infectious disease that causes the victim to cough violently. Also know as TB or consumption, the disease was the most common killer of colonists at one time.

Wet-nurse A woman who breastfeeds the baby of another woman. Wet-nurses have usually just had children of their own, so they are producing milk.

1500

1585 The first British colony in America is established by Sir Walter Raleigh at Roanoke Island, Virginia (North Carolina today). The colony only lasts a year, but further attempts are made to settle in the same place.

1587 Virginia Dare is the first child to be born of English parents in America. She is born in the colony of Roanoke on August 18.

1595 Pocahontas is born in Virginia, daughter of Chief Powhatan.

ABOVE: **Massasoit, or Ousamequin, chief of the Wampanoag of Massachusetts and Rhode Island, pays a friendly visit to the Pilgrims' camp at Plymouth Colony with his warriors.**

1600

1607 Jamestown becomes the first colony in Virginia. It is established by the London Company.

1608 The first women arrive in Jamestown, Virginia.

1616 Pocahontas dies in Gravesend, England, aged 22 years.

1619 Twenty Africans are brought to Jamestown, Virginia, to work as indentured servants.

1620 The *Mayflower* lands at Cape Cod on November 9. One hundred and two people are on board, and later that year they establish the colony at Plymouth Plantation.

1630 A large Puritan colony is set up in Massachusetts Bay.

1634 The first settlement is established in Maryland, by Catholics.

1638 Anne Hutchinson is banished from Massachusetts by the Puritan governors for her religious views.

1650 Anne Bradstreet becomes the first American women poet to be published, with her collection of poems called *The Tenth Muse Lately Sprung up in America, by a Gentlewoman of Those Parts.*

1652 The first antislavery laws are written in Rhode Island, making the practice illegal.

1660 June 1, Mary Dyer is hanged on Boston Common for her religious beliefs. She becomes a martyr to the Quaker cause

1664 Laws are passed in Maryland making slaves bound to serve for life unless they can buy their freedom. This law is then passed in other colonies, including New York and Virginia.

1681 The colony of Pennsylvania is established, named after its leader William Penn. It is a Quaker colony.

1692 The Salem witch trials take place in Massachusetts. Between June and September 150 people are accused of witchcraft, and 14 women and 6 men are executed.

1700

1800

1700 Samuel Sewall writes *The Sin of Slaveholding*.

1765 A Stamp Tax is imposed on America by Britain, and the colonies oppose it by agreeing not to import any more British goods.

1773 The Boston Tea Party. English tea is thrown into the harbor at Boston in protest against taxes.

1773 Phillis Wheatley becomes the first published black woman poet and the first black author in America with her collection of poetry called *Poems on Various Subjects, Religious and Moral*, published in England.

1774 On October 25 Penelope Barker of Edenton, North Carolina, invites 50 of her friends to a tea party where they sign a document stating they would support the quest for independence from Britain.

1775–1783 The Revolutionary War.

1776 The Declaration of Independence is signed.

1785 Martha Ballard, a midwife, starts writing her diary in Hallowell, Maine.

1787 The U.S. Constitution is written.

1790 Judith Sargent Stevens Murray writes her book *On the Equality of the Sexes*.

1792 Mary Wollstonecraft's *A Vindication of the Rights of Women* is published in England.

1812 Ruth Pease starts writing her diary in Blandford, Massachusetts.

ABOVE: **Boatloads of people waving farewell to the *Mayflower* as it leaves Plymouth, England, for America, September 6, 1620.**

BOOKS

Berkin, Carol, *First Generations: Women in Colonial America*, New York: Hill and Wang, 1997.

Calloway, Colin G., *The World Turned Upside Down : Indian Voices from Early America (The Bedford Series in History and Culture)*, Boston: Bedford/St. Martins, 1994.

Clark, Beth, and Arthur M Schlesinger Jr. (Senior Consulting Editor), *Anne Hutchinson: Religious Leader*, Northborough, Mass.: Chelsea House Publications, 2000.

Collins, Gail, *America's Women: 400 Years of Dolls, Drudges, Helpmates and Heroines*, New York: William Morrow, 2003.

Cott, Nancy F. (ed.), *No Small Courage: A History of Women in the United States*, New York, Oxford University Press, 2000.

Heinemann, Sue, *The New York Public Library Amazing Women in American History*, New York: Stonesong Press, 1999.

Kerber, Linda K., and Jane Sherron De Hart (eds.), *Women's America: Refocusing the Past*, New York: Oxford University Press, 1995.

Kierner, Cynthia A., *Beyond the Household: Women's Place in the Early South, 1700-1835*, New York: Cornell University Press, 1998.

Lutz, Norma Jean, and Arthur M Schlesinger Jr. (Senior Consulting Editor), *Cotton Mather: Author, Clergyman and Scholar* Northborough, Mass.: Chelsea House Publications, 2000.

McGill, Alice, *Molly Bannaky*, New York: Houghton Mifflin Company, 1999.

WEBSITES

"A Briefe and True Report of the New Found Land of Virginia"
http://www.blackmask.com/books63c/7nflvdex.htm

"American Centuries: View from New England"
http://memorialhall.mass.edu/home.html

"American Women's History: A Research Guide"
http://frank.mtsu.edu/~kmiddlet/history/women.html

"Camps and Firesides of the Revolution"
http://www.blackmask.com/books42c/campfiresdex.htm

"Early Modern Women Database"
http://www.lib.umd.edu/ETC/LOCAL/emw/emw.php3

"History's Women"
http://www.historyswomen.com/

"Incidents in the Life of a Slave Girl"
http://afroamhistory.about.com/library/bljacobs_contents.htm

"National Women's Hall of Fame"
http://www.greatwomen.org/

Page numbers in italic indicate illustrations or maps.
Those in bold indicate volume numbers.

Index by Marian Anderson